Diving for
Peter Throckmorton

Treasure
A Studio Book · The Viking Press · New York

Copyright © Peter Throckmorton 1965, 1969, 1977
All rights reserved
First published in 1977 by The Viking Press
625 Madison Avenue, New York, N.Y. 10022
Published simultaneously in Canada by
Penguin Books Canada Limited

Portions of this book appeared in *National Geographic* and *Archaeology*.

Library of Congress Cataloging in Publication Data
Throckmorton, Peter.
   Diving for treasure.
   (A Studio book)
   Bibliography: p.
   Includes index.
   1. Underwater archaeology. 2. Shipwrecks.
I. Title.
CC77.U5T46   622′.19   77–6689
ISBN 0-670-27449-6

Printed in the United States of America

Title page: *Diver surveys the amphora mound of the Kyrenia ship.*

Contents

Preface **6**

Where to Begin **20**

The Birth of Marine Archaeology **30**

The Wrecks and Their Whereabouts **46**

The Divers **66**

The Treasures **78**

Simple Underwater Surveying and Photography **100**

Reconstructing an Ancient Shipwreck **114**

Treasure Diving and Politics **122**

Afterword **124**

Bibliographical Note **131**

Acknowledgments **132**

Photo Credits **133**

Index **134**

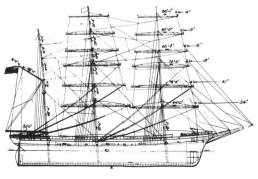

Preface

Ships have fascinated me ever since I began to play with small rubber ones in the bathtub. I have often asked myself, why this attraction? Ancestors, perhaps—I was born into a family that is proud to trace itself to Norman beginnings. If disease can be transmitted through one's genes from generation to generation, then surely a feeling for ships can come to one in much the same way. Certainly there would seem to be evidence that my sea madness is hereditary, as it must be among virtually all northern peoples.

When I was a small child, my first school composition concerned a shipwreck. This passion for wrecks was accentuated by the great hurricane that swept up America's East Coast in 1938, littering the beaches in front of my family's Long Island summer home with fascinating wreckage. I collected lobster pots and dory oars and pot markers with individual markings until the porch overflowed and my mother had had enough!

Then there were the schooners, heartbreakingly beautiful in their last days, commandeered by old, proud men who were sometimes kind to a sail-struck ten-year-old. When I was old enough, I was sent to a yacht club to learn to sail dinghies, the exercise thought vital to a young man's proper summer training. I resisted, feeling, with fine snobbishness, that those athletic boys with their dinghies had no more genuine interest in the sea than I in their bourgeois concerns. After all, what purpose could be served by tacking up and down Long Island Sound when one could tramp on a downeast square-rigger's deck and hear the ghostly echo of Cape Horn gales, past the croaking of the frogs where she lay abandoned? Who should care to sail to Block Island in a silly race when the West Indies beckoned?

In spite of all the efforts of my united family to steer me into the world of yachting and its middle-class comforts, the heroes of my youth were the fishermen and the schoonermen I met. When, at the age of sixteen, I decided to run away to sea, I was almost consciously trying to mold my life into a pattern that imitated that of Alan Villiers, Joseph Conrad, and Felix Riesenberg, my favorite sea-story writers, and to create a meaningful identity from what seemed to me a meaningless future. In short, I wanted to partake in the making of the history of the sea.

Years later, while I was still pursuing that romantic dream somewhere in the Pacific, I came across Captain Jacques-Yves Cousteau's first *National Geographic* article about the Roman and Greek ships he had found and excavated in the Mediterranean. He and his crew were fascinated by the traces of those long-dead Roman mariners—their own remote ancestors. And when I myself was skipper of a large yacht and lady passengers harped on how I must love the sea, my perennial comment to them was, "Why should I love something that has been trying its best to kill me for thirty years!" What I really loved, and what fascinates me still, is the profession of seagoing.

The world of small ships in which I was brought up is greatly misunderstood, often by its own practitioners. Small-ship seamen—and by that I mean those who habitually work in coasters of 499 gross registered tons and under,[1] are misunderstood for many reasons. Principally, this type of seagoing is a profession that is most often learned by inarticulate men. Seamanship cannot be learned from a book: scholars, however knowledgeable, can never really understand the sea without experiencing her. It is no coincidence that Conrad, Villiers, and Riesenberg were all shipmasters. Conrad best of all has described the semi-piratical world of the small owner-skipper in his descriptions

---

[1] *499 GRT is an arbitrary limiting size for certain licensing arrangements, and ships that exceed that size must have better-qualified crews and more complicated and expensive life-saving equipment, among other requirements.*

Shipwreck of the Determinée.

The Kaiulani was the last American-built square-rigged ship. Constructed as a three-masted bark at the turn of the century in Bath, Maine, she remained anchored in San Francisco for many years until the beginning of World War II, when she was recommissioned to sail to Australia. There the American Army cut her down into a barge for use in New Guinea. The pictures of Kaiulani at sea were taken by Karl Kortum, then an adventurous college student who sailed her as an ordinary seaman, now director of the San Francisco Maritime Museum.

Kaiulani *ended her working days as a log barge in the Philippines. She was eventually scrapped, but the United States Navy returned significant parts of her to San Francisco, where they will form a central part of a new park. The struggle to save* Kaiulani, *which ended with less than complete success, nonetheless marked the beginning of a new ship-preservation movement in America.*

The California gold rush brought into being the American clipper ship, designed to dash around Cape Horn in the shortest possible time. The first such clippers were smallish ships, of six or eight hundred tons and a bit over one hundred and fifty feet long, like Snow Squall (this page, bottom), whose remains now lie in Port Stanley Harbor, the Falkland Islands. One of the two only surviving relics of an age that made America famous, Snow Squall was built in 1851 near Portland, Maine.

One year later, Donald McKay was building the most sophisticated and fastest wooden sailing ships ever made, including Glory of the Seas (this page, top), that could travel twenty-two (land) miles an hour with a cargo of two thousand tons.

Sailing bulk carriers built of steel, like the Champigny (opposite page, top), represent man's last attempt to make sailing ships pay. Built in France in 1902, she could carry over three thousand tons of cargo. When the French government stopped subsidizing sailing ships, she was sold to the Finns, who renamed her Fennia. Dismasted off Cape Horn in 1927, she fetched up in Port Stanley, where she remained as a storage hulk until 1967 when she was purchased by a wealthy San Francisco businessman who intended to tow her back home to use as a floating restaurant. Alas, he ran out of money in 1972, and the magnificent old ship was stripped for scrapping by a shipyard that did not get paid on time. She is now an abandoned hulk in the River Uruguay (opposite page, bottom).

of Lingard. What people don't understand is that the Lingards of the world still exist today, slightly transformed by the advent of the diesel engine.

I saw my first sunken ship in 1946 and experienced my first feelings of fear: giant octopuses, sharks, *ghosts*—how wondrous it was! When the aqualung arrived, in the early 1950s, I became professionally involved in nautical archaeology and have been ever since.

Unfortunately, many people who wish to study sunken ships are often called treasure seekers. For me, there is only one true treasure in the hundreds of thousands of wrecks that are scattered on the ocean floor: the ships—more mysterious than the pyramids of Egypt and as expressive, bearing witness to man's eternal ingenuity.

Nearly everyone involved in this special world is continually engaged in a fencing match with authority. Whether or not anything is done illegally, the authorities invariably believe that deviation was somehow involved. They have good reason for thinking as they do: most small-ship seamen are in violation of some law or other. The reason is not that they are criminally minded, but simply that they are surrounded by such a web of regulations—many nonsensical—that it is nearly impossible to operate a small ship without being vulnerable to authority's abuses. This situation, combined with a militant seamen's union, has pretty well abolished non-government-subsidized shipping in the United States, and the same process is well under way in Britain. As a result, sailors are reluctant when confronted by authority; shipwrights are the same.

The situation is the same today as it was in Homeric times, when the identical situation existed in slightly more spectacular form. This is why Roman writers, for instance, who wrote best about the different aspects of their contemporary world—that is, the engineer Vitruvius, the politician Petronius, and the poet Juvenal—in their writings of seamen and ships, all sound remarkably like prewar lady writers from New York describing Nantucket fishermen. There is, in fact, only one description of the great imperial grain ships that connected Rome and her Egyptian empire, written by a Greek who happened to visit one that had been driven to Athens by bad weather. It reads for all the world like *The New York Times* correspondent's account of the first visit of the *Queen Mary* to New York: long on local color and short on the workings of the ship. It is no coincidence that only one first-rate writer in English has written convincingly about marine engineering: Rudyard Kipling, who also wrote of fishing and soldiering.

We have remarkably little good oral history recorded from the 1930s, when the last old-fashioned ships were disappearing along with the skippers who could man them. Part of the reason for this oversight is the fact that few people realized that the men and the ships were truly disappearing forever. (Also, there were no earnest graduate students doing Ph.D.'s on sea traditions.) It was generally believed that ships should be left to technicians and not to social historians. In any case, in 1938, the tape recorder had not yet been invented and oral history in one's own backyard was a startling idea. The main reason, I think, that so little was recorded is that nearly all the old boys who knew schooners and fishing avoided writers like the plague—many of them had a background of rumrunning and were fearful of government persecution.

It is no wonder, then, that a whole world has slipped away from us, almost without our noticing. Sailing ships were an expression of the technology and civilization of their times. Like Greek temples they were built with unbelievable skill, with sophisti-

cated traditional techniques, and with a supreme respect for the materials and the sea. If one is to have an understanding of how the world was shaped by these ships, it would seem desirable to attempt to understand the ships themselves. I am sure that tens of thousands of people who would not normally have thought of or understood the saga of American whaling and Herman Melville's masterpiece, *Moby Dick*, have understood after visiting the schooner *Charles Morgan*, enshrined at Mystic Seaport, Connecticut.

In 1921 Samuel Eliot Morison, our greatest maritime historian, wrote:

Never, in these United States, has the brain of man conceived, nor the hand of man fashioned, so perfect a thing as the clipper ship. In her, the long-suppressed artistic impulse of a practical, hard-worked race burst into flower. The *Flying Cloud* was our Rheims, the *Sovereign of the Seas* our Parthenon, the *Lightning* our Amiens; but they were monuments carved from snow. For a brief moment of time they flashed their splendor around the world, then disappeared with the sudden completeness of the wild pigeon.[1]

Moving lines, yet *Glory of the Seas*, the last masterpiece from the hand of the great artist of clipper ships, Donald McKay, who also designed, in the 1850s, *Flying Cloud*, *Sovereign of the Seas*, and *Lightning*, was burned for her copper on the West Coast a year after Morison wrote them. How can we be so indifferent to our heritage of ships? Even in the 1830s, after four hundred years of Turkish occupation, the Greeks were aware enough of their cultural heritage to protest successfully the conversion of the Parthenon into a palace for their new Bavarian king!

[1] *Maritime History of Massachusetts.* Boston, 1921 (pp. 370–371).

Joseph Conrad's first command was the little British bark Otago *(far left, above), aboard which the action described in his novel* The Secret Sharer *is set.* Otago *was scrapped in 1942. Only three ships of the same type exist in the world. One of them is the* Elissa, *shown under sail as the Norwegian* Fjeld *(above) and in the slip in Piraeus, Greece (center), where she is being prepared for her voyage to Galveston, Texas. Once in Galveston, she will be restored to her former glory for museum exhibition.*

The surviving square-rigged ocean wanderers are going very fast. There are only four reasonably intact ocean-sailing ships from the mid-nineteenth century left; three of these are in the Falkland Islands, where they have miraculously survived after being abandoned there more than one hundred years ago. They are the *Jhelum*, a British East Indiaman of 1849; the *Charles Cooper*, a Western Ocean Packet ship built in 1856; and the 1841 British-built *Vicar of Bray*, the last surviving veteran of the California gold rush. As I write these lines, plans are being formed that will, it is hoped, make it possible to preserve these ships for posterity.

Up to the beginning of World War II the backwaters of the maritime world were clogged with abandoned sailing ships that were, for good commercial reasons, scrapped or burned or otherwise disposed of. Today there are perhaps only between forty and fifty square-rigged ships of pre-1914 vintage afloat. Of these, about twenty are stabilized in permanent homes. Twenty others are in danger of being scrapped in the fairly near future. More than twenty important sailing ships have been scrapped in the past ten years.

These include the famous *Lawhill*, the lovely *British Isles*, the *Pax* in Noumea, and the *Mary Moore*.

Through the initiative of the San Francisco Maritime Museum, the *Polly Woodside*, once known as the prettiest bark ever built in Belfast, has been saved in Tasmania. Alexander Hall's lovely little boat *Elissa*, the world's last surviving ship that closely resembles Joseph Conrad's first command, the *Otago*, is now laid up in Piraeus. I am proud to say that I am her last master of register, in a chain that began with an obscure Liverpool shipowner named Henry Fowler Watt in 1878.

The situation in the Mediterranean concerning ancient ships is, if possible, worse. No Mediterranean country has managed to preserve them or even to produce usable drawings of their remains before they dried to dust. Marine archaeology has been left largely to ignorant men, by authorities whose ignorance is less excusable, because the divers, after all, are not necessarily trained to be archaeologists. After thirty years of destruction by skin divers, a strong movement is being led by divers in the south of France to forbid unqualified divers to pick at the wrecks. These men have been mostly inspired by the superlative work that has been done in Scandinavia by Lars Barkman and Ole Crumlin Peterson, and in Cyprus by Michael Katsev, who excavated, preserved, and exhibited a beautiful fifty-foot merchant ship from the time of Alexander the Great. After seven years of devoted effort and the expenditure of a huge sum of money, his project was suspended by the 1974 Turkish invasion of Kyrenia.

The photographs in this book are a record of nearly thirty years of my own personal search for lost ships. For the most part, I have kept the narrative to what I have seen and experienced myself.

On the following pages an attempt is made to give some firsthand insights into what the problems are. To me, the exploration and reconstruction of the lost world of the ancient mariners is a far greater treasure than the actual loot that has been brought up from the depths of the sea. It is my conviction that it is technically possible to reconstruct a ship from carefully studied insignificant pieces, and that the most interesting artifact in a shipwreck is, usually, the ship itself.

A few—a very few—treasure hunters have become rich. Most, being dreamers, have gone broke and quit or have become amateur archaeologists. Conversely, the father of archaeology, Heinrich Schliemann, took care to become rich before he went treasure hunting. He knew that this pastime, this obsession, this mania—or whatever else treasure hunting might be—becomes more and more expensive the deeper into it one sinks. The same, and even more so, holds true of diving for sunken treasures. But treasure hunting there must be, whether the hunt is for gold or wood; as with land excavations, marine archaeology can answer dozens—hundreds—of questions central to the understanding of the history of man.

Built in England in 1841 for the specialized trade of carrying copper ore from Chile for smelting in England, The Vicar of Bray *(see also page 33), along with* Snow Squall, *survives thousands of ships that sailed for California when gold was discovered. She now lies in Goose Green, the Falkland Islands, although the National Maritime Historical Society hopes to return her to San Francisco, where she will form the centerpiece of a new maritime museum dedicated to the memory of what Karl Kortum called "the greatest movement of man since the Crusades: the 1849 California gold rush."*

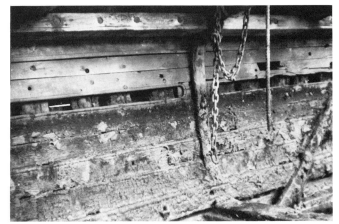

In 1969, a distinguished group of Englishmen resolved to "bring back from the other side of the world, recondition and put on display the most historic modern ship in the world." One year later the S.S. Great Britain was returned to Bristol, from which she had been originally launched in 1843. These pictures were taken a few months after her arrival.

Designed and built by Isambard Kingdom Brunel, the great Victorian engineer who also built the Great Eastern, she was the first modern transatlantic steamer. She was eventually converted into a sailing ship and fetched up in the Falklands like so many others. She had lain abandoned in Whalebone Bay, near Port Stanley, from 1937 until 1965, when Karl Kortum began to study her. Kortum was able to persuade millionaire Jack Hayward to put up the money for her return to England.

Where to Begin

Diving and Diving Gear

The greatest romance of the sea is, perhaps, danger. Diving itself is easy; the dangers of the so-called deep are simple, but hazards there certainly are, and if you are not well prepared, they will get you as inevitably as the traffic on a four-lane highway will eliminate the drunk who casually wanders across during rush hour.

Rules of aqualung diving are taught at local YMCAs, as well as at numerous other places. The general rule to remember about all diving is that the practical limit of underwater work on compressed air is about two hundred feet, although it is possible to go as deep as three hundred feet without passing out. Given enough money, divers can dive to one thousand feet on mixed gases—by replacing the nitrogen in the air mixture with helium, and the like.

One of the most useful technical guides on diving is the *U.S. Navy Diving Manual*, easily obtainable from the Government Printing Office in Washington, D.C.

In England and America diving has become so popular that divers must have certificates before they can buy equipment or get their tanks filled. These are issued after courses and examinations by the British Sub Aqua Club in England and in the United States by the National Association of Underwater Instructors, as well as affiliated organizations.

Divers obviously need good gear and the knowledge of how and when to use it. Personally, I find discussions as to whether the Brand A gadget is superior to the Brand B an unnecessary bore. There are approximately one dozen diving-gear manufacturers in the world. They all use the Cousteau Gagnan patent, and all their products *work*.

At the time I was learning to photograph, Robert Capa, the late, great photojournalist, counseled me on the art of photographing with these words: "First you get a competent camera, then you learn to take competent photographs, and, when you look at the photographs, *you will know*."

The diver should select his equipment in much the same manner; if he acquires competent diving gear and learns to use it, he will know what is best for him. But beware; if the diver approaches the sea with equipment that he has erroneously calculated to be competent, he will suffer the same fate as the audacious fly that licks jam off the palm of one's hand!

Good diving equipment begins with a bottle of compressed air, at a pressure that can be as high as three thousand pounds per square inch, though it is often less. Air is metered to the diver through a regulating device that takes the high-pressure air in the bottle and reduces it to low pressure. The low-pressure air is then metered at ambient pressure—that is, at the pressure of the sea around the diver—by a clever little diaphragm valve device. This device derives from the gasogene regulators originally designed by the French engineer Emile Gagnan for delivering carbon gas to automotive engines as a substitute for gasoline. It was Cousteau who recognized the possibility that this gadget could regulate the air pressure in a bottle to deliver air to a diver.

The key to all diving, then, is pressure. Water is heavy. The air we breathe is under pressure, as air has weight. The sea has weight as well, and the air that man breathes into the sea must be delivered to him at the pressure of the sea around him. The pressure required increases at the rate of an additional 14.7 pounds per square inch for every 33 feet of depth. Thus, as the diver descends, his air supply must increase in pressure. (Theoretically, man can dive to the

---

A diver learns to clear her mask in water. Holding the top of the mask, she blows air from her nose, and water flows out the bottom of the mask. Today's diving equipment is so simple that most people can learn to dive after a few hours of competent instruction.

very abyss as long as the air-filled spaces in his body are filled with gas at equivalent pressure.)

The problems of pressure have occupied the minds of scientists for more than a century, ever since the great Louis Boutan subjected a viper to pressure for a day and then released the pressure. The viper died in convulsions, and Boutan was able to see why: a bubble of gas was visible in the reptile's eye. Gas killed the viper and could just as easily kill man if he were to be subjected to and then relieved of pressure. More than anything else, it is the little bubbles of nitrogen that kill divers.

Above: *Filming at the Great Basses Reef.* Top right: *Underwater excavation of an ancient ship requires a great amount of gear. Here, at Pelagos, a cement platform was built on an island near the wreck to support the heavy-duty air compressors that fill our air bottles and a recompression chamber facility.*

Right: *A well-dressed Mediterranean diver, Nikos Kartelias has been chief diver on many of our expeditions. He wears a "half" neoprene jacket, a diving knife strapped to his left leg, a pressure-activated depth gauge on his left wrist, and a belt with a quick-release buckle. Seventy pounds of air bottles, which become slightly buoyant in water, are carried on his back.*

Basic Diving Gear
1. Tank of compressed air
2. Regulator
3. Pair of fins
4. Mask
5. Belt, with about 5 pounds of lead
5. Snorkel
6. Neoprene rubber suit (in cold water)

Choosing a Diving Boat

If you intend to explore many sites and live in far deserted reefs and islands, a ship is required. Once the wreck you are out to explore is found, the ship probably becomes a liability if it is possible to camp on the shore and use a diving barge as a diving platform.

Whether you are working in the English Channel, the Caribbean, the Mediterranean, the Red Sea, or the South Pacific, the ship you choose must be a life-support system—a good ship of whatever type, fishing boat or yacht. Yachts usually won't do as well as working boats as they have relatively little working space for the size of the ship. The primary requirement for any working boat is space.

The diving boat must be as comfortable as possible for a crew of from six to twelve people. She has to have decent bunks (that don't leak in any weather), sleepable during any time of day in the area where the boat is working. She has to have a galley that will not drive the cook to mutiny, and a mess room where everyone can eat comfortably and sit after meals to write letters, read, or drink coffee. If you are in the tropics or subtropics in the summer, your boat must have a good awning that protects people on deck from the sun. In fact, you will find that, moored over a wreck site, in nearly any ocean, you and your crew will spend nearly all your time on deck.

The general rule of thumb must be that your boat is a tool, and the simpler she is, the better. Fancy boats, of any type, just generally won't do; they are too complicated and too expensive. The engineer has enough equipment to worry about on a diving boat without being tormented by hot-water systems and pressure air tanks and all the nonsense in today's big twin-screw cruiser engine rooms.

I have worked with many diving boats, and I've learned only that generalizations about boats are meaningless. My own two little research vessels, *Archangel*, a converted Greek cargo ship, and *Stormie Seas*, a modified Greek island trading schooner, worked as well as any. They were both about fifty feet on deck, with double-ended hulls, good anchors and mooring gear, and all the living facilities listed above. They both had adequate deck space, *Stormie Seas* more than *Archangel*. *Archangel* lacked storage, tanks, and ballast space, which we found to be a seri-

Diver Costas Mangouros with our recompression chamber. A bank of emergency compressed-air bottles is in the background.

ous disadvantage. These little vessels have probably done more expedition time than any other little ships afloat, so they have more than earned their keep. A boat much smaller than either of them would be too small, and a boat much larger would be too expensive and difficult to handle.

Research

Local newspaper files are a prime source of wreck information. Once you know that a ship went down on a given date, there are literally dozens of ways to expand your research. Lloyds Register or the ABS and Veritas registers will give you the date, dimensions, and construction material of the vessel. The insurance company that covered the vessel might have a copy of her manifest. It is remarkable how soon vessels are abandoned and forgotten after the insurance has been paid. Professional salvage is so expensive that only the most obvious wrecks were salvaged in the days of professional helmet diving. Wrecks that salvagers abandoned fifty years ago, for instance, can often be purchased for a few hundred dollars today. This is especially true in England, where diving clubs have purchased from the legal owners and found many World War I and II wrecks and made good money out of the bronze scrap they salvaged. I have one acquaintance who is searching for a World War II cargo ship that has on board more than a million dollars' worth of copper telephone wire, at scrap value, which was never salvaged because she lay very deep. The equation is simple: scrap value of the copper minus cost of salvage operation equals possible profit.

One example of a very successful commercial treasure search is the salvage of the British passenger liner *Egypt*, run down and sunk in the Bay of Biscay during World War I. *Egypt* was carrying millions of dollars in gold bullion. A brilliant Italian named Quaglia made an agreement with Lloyds to find her, which he did in six hundred feet of water in one of the most dangerous areas of the world. Quaglia made himself a millionaire. He developed a whole deep-diving technology for the *Egypt* job that, fifty years later, is still probably the most practical for straight commercial salvage of very deep wrecks. Divers in observation chambers directed grabs from the surface by telephone until the strong room was reached and nearly all the gold salvaged. The *Niagara*, sunk by a Japanese submarine off Australia, carried a similar cargo. She too was salvaged in approximately the same way.

One friend has made the acquaintance of the skippers of local sports fishing boats who take groups out to fish on weekends. Wrecks are, in effect, artificial reefs that attract swarms of fish. Charter-boat skippers make their living on their ability to take their clients to good fishing grounds. Now that loran, the long-range radio equipment, has made offshore navigation to within about fifty feet simple, it is possible for the charter boats to return to the same wreck weekend after weekend. The loran bearings are a jealously guarded professional secret, but my friend has convinced the skippers that he can be trusted and has now located and explored hundreds of wrecks—clipper ships, German submarines, torpedoed tankers, and freighters—with their help.

Trawler skippers are good acquaintances for a diver to cultivate, because they make an art of dragging their nets near wrecks, where fish are likely to swarm. As a hung net can cost tens of thousands of dollars, they have to know exact locations. Modern wrecks of big ships are often festooned with lost nets. The Italian group led by Bruno Vailati that filmed the wreck of the *Andrea Doria* were frightened by sharks, the depth, and the presence of that mighty ship, but what bothered them most were the festoons of nylon "ghost nets," eternally fishing in the dark depths of the Atlantic. Northern wreck divers carry sharp knives, not so much against sharks but as insurance against getting caught in a strong nylon net.

Funding

All adventurers, whether explorers, treasure hunters, or archaeologists, know that raising sufficient funds for any venture is far more arduous a task than any they will encounter during the expedition itself. Most well-conducted expeditions are more healthy than adventurous; once an adventure occurs, it is symptomatic that the expedition itself is beginning to fall apart.

Few individuals, however, have the money to support a serious long-term expedition. There are two money markets for work underwater to which the would-be expedition leader can turn; if the expedition is in search of something that has scientific value and if the expedition is supported by a recognized institution, such as a university or a museum, the fund raiser's problem is somewhat easier. In some countries it is possible for individuals to take tax deductions for donations to charitable foundations, making it easier for the would-be explorer to approach a foundation. There are all kinds of foundations. In America they are conveniently described in the *Foundation Directory*, a twenty-five-dollar tome published annually.

There are many pitfalls, however. One encountered by Admiral Byrd is typical: one well-known name not on the map of Antarctica made by Byrd is that of Lydia Pinkham. Her heirs were willing to help finance Byrd on condition that he name a mountain after the maker of the famous female elixir. Byrd refused, although he was in sore need of the money.

If the expedition is a pure treasure-hunting venture, then the would-be expedition leader is limited to investments in a joint venture by individuals, just as in any other business venture. The trouble is that there are so many charlatans in the treasure business that it's hard to get funded like a business because too many people have gotten burned.

If one really has a good treasure location, there are said to be various gentlemen in Florida who will invest.

The problem of money will always be with us. If I have made a contribution to the field, it is the adaptation of simple everyday tools to underwater work—that is, being able to work cheaply.

The major financial problem of ship excavation is conservation of the artifacts found. The field is full of horror stories of expedition leaders who carried out their excavation and then faced the fact that no one would pay for conservation. The worst case of this is the American schooner *Alvin Clark*, found intact at the bottom of Lake Michigan, where she had lain since before the Civil War. She was raised to be a museum exhibit and is now rotting away because no one had realized that she required sophisticated preservation before she could be stable.

It seems that donors attracted by the idea of discovery and exploration are not so enthusiastic when it comes time to conserve the finds. Once his journey is financed, the explorer would do well to think ahead: "Will there be money to save what I find?"

Archangel (right) *was built in 1946 to carry fruit from the island of Poros to Salonika. Here she is moored over the second-century-*A.D. *wreck at Torre Sgaratta, near Taranto, Italy.* Above: *Under sail in a gentle breeze,* Stormie Seas *is manned by students of the 1975 Ocean Science Association summer seminar. Her generous deck space is unusual for a sailing boat her size.*

Overleaf, left: Stormie Seas, *with all sails set, on a charter cruise off the coast of Turkey. She is the last traditional Greek schooner. Still under sail,* Stormie Seas *has provided dozens of students with a glimpse of the life led by Mediterranean mariners in the days before engines were invented.*

Overleaf, right: Evangelistria of Mykonos *was built by Mavrikos of Syros in 1938 as a cargo schooner. She used her sails until 1961, when this picture was taken. In 1977, she was still carrying cargo (under power) from Mykonos to Piraeus. She stands at the end of a Greek island tradition that goes back at least one thousand years.*

The Birth of Marine Archaeology

The first scientific dives employing mechanical equipment were made in 1844 by Henri Milne Edwards, a French professor of zoology. This pioneer effort took place two years after the first successful salvage job—using the newly developed Siebe German helmet diving apparatus—was made, and almost one hundred years before another Frenchman, Jacques-Yves Cousteau, made the first experimental dives with the aqualung, the device that has at last opened the shallow waters of the world to exploration by man.

During the first hundred years of diving, the sea admitted man only as a fleeting visitor, one who snatched what he could and surfaced as quickly as possible. He was a hero; "deep-sea diver" evoked an image of uncommon bravery and skill. Though the old magic is gone, it has been replaced by the new magical possibilities of living underwater for extended periods and becoming a true inhabitant of the bottom of the sea. With this development came the ability to carry out complex and highly technical activities with standards as demanding as those normally used on land.

Field archaeology became a science when the antiquarians of the late nineteenth century began to realize, as O. G. S. Crawford, one of the earliest English archaeologists, noted, that it was not the object in isolation which revealed the past, but the object in relation to its original surroundings. "A Roman coin picked up in a field is evidence of nothing but a hole in a Roman tunic; but one found under the undisturbed rampart . . . was proof that the rampart had been built after the coin was lost, and must therefore be Roman or later. . . . That sounds simple and obvious enough, but so do many things after a genius has invented them."

Like the first land digs, early underwater excavations were carried out in order to recover specific objects for their intrinsic value. They were not, in the contemporary archaeological sense, excavations, but rather salvage jobs.

After the end of World War II, when free diving became a popular sport, skin divers began to find old wrecks by the dozens, especially in the waters of the French and Italian Riviera and the Florida Keys. In 1950 Professor Nino Lamboglia began working on a Roman cargo ship of the first century A.D. The wreck lay in one hundred and forty feet of water at the mouth of a river off Albenga, on the Italian Riviera. Silt from the river had covered and preserved much of the hull of the sunken ship. For generations it had been known to the local fishermen, who found examples of the amphorae, the ship's main cargo, in their nets.

Lamboglia began excavating the wreck with a clam shell bucket, but found it necessary to develop more careful methods when wood from the wreck began to surface. By 1958 he had developed a system that combined photography with a steel frame set out on the bottom, allowing divers to record each object in place before it was raised.

In 1952 Captain Cousteau undertook to excavate the wreck of another Roman cargo ship off a rocky islet known as Le Grand Congloué, near Marseilles. He raised hundreds of amphorae from the main cargo of the ship, and parts of the ship itself. Then, in 1958, Commander Philippe Taillez, who succeeded Cousteau as commander of the French Navy's Undersea Research Group, headed another excavation at the Titan reef off Marseilles. Four amphorae salvaged from that wreck were dated to the first century A.D.

Both Taillez and Professor Fernand Benoit, the consulting archaeologist during Cousteau's Grand Congloué excavation, concluded that the proper aim of a ship excavation was the reconstruction of the ship itself, and that better methods would have to be developed before technically correct underwater excavations became possible. The fact that the object's relationship to its surroundings was the primary means of discovering the past was nowhere better demonstrated than in these excavations. It soon became obvious that the object of greatest value was the ship itself, and equally obvious that the ship could never be raised as a whole.

Few areas of historical scholarship are as lacking in physical evidence as the history of naval architecture. Already we find it difficult to imagine the ships described by naval historians in the early nineteenth century. The terminology of Nelson's navy is rapidly becoming obscure. Records written earlier than the 1600s scarcely exist. The student then becomes involved with "logical" reconstructions of the ships in which the great sea commanders of history sailed. No one really knows what kind of galleys formed Themisticles' fleet at Salamis, or exactly what the *Santa Maria* looked like.

Theoretical reconstructions of ships depend on secondary sources, such as the base of the Winged Victory of Samothrace in the Louvre, on which is carved a fourth century B.C. bireme. Many books are filled with speculations about ancient ships and their tentative reconstructions; some are better than others, but the best is only an informed guess, a poor substitute for a set of plans. And though the ships themselves exist, little attention was paid to them during early experiments in underwater archaeology.

American involvement in underwater archaeology began in 1960, when the University of Pennsylvania Museum sent an expedition to Turkey to excavate the wreck of a ship of c. 1200 B.C. George Bass was director of the expedition, and I was technical adviser. Joan DuPlat Taylor, who had been Director of Antiquities in Cyprus and who later founded the Institute of Nautical Archaeology in England, was archaeologist in charge.

The wreck lay ninety feet down, off a cluster of small islands near Cape Gelidonya in south Turkey. Almost nothing was visible except bits of the flat copper ingots that comprised the ship's main cargo. We decided to make a detailed plan of what remained of the more than three-thousand-year-old wreck, then to excavate everything that remained of the ship and its cargo in such a manner that reconstruction on paper would be possible.

The crew we recruited for the job consisted almost entirely of technicians: draftsmen, photographers, and archaeologists selected because of their specific skills. Diving was new to nearly half of them, but it was far easier to train healthy, skilled technicians to dive than it was to make specialists out of divers. The only member of the crew who had previously participated in an underwater archaeological excavation was Frederic Dumas, of the French Navy's Undersea Research Group, who had been chief diver with Cousteau and had been personally involved in the development of much of the equipment we were using. The basic crew consisted of eighteen people, nine in the archaeological crew and nine Turkish boatmen, four of whom were experienced helmet divers.

The job we meant to do required a photographic darkroom, a drafting room large enough for two draftsmen, laboratory space for cleaning and preserving recovered material, space for high- and low-pressure air compressors and for the repair and maintenance of machinery, and a large supply of fresh water for soaking copper and bronze objects. All this required much more space than that available on any ship we could afford on our limited budget. We therefore built a camp on the nearest beach where fresh water was available, and we worked from Turkish fishing boats.

Originally we had planned to use a drafting-photographic frame system for charting the wreck, but the irregular nature of the rocky bottom made this difficult. We settled on the tape triangulation method. A series of fixed points were marked with steep pitons driven into the rock, and measurements were made of each major object from not less than three of them. As a check on the results of triangulation and measured drawings made on the bottom, a series of mosaic photographs were made by a photographer swimming at a fixed distance over the bottom. Each frame had a meter rod attached, and when enlargements were made the scale could be checked from it. Drawings were never made from the photographs themselves.

The ship had carried a tinker or metalsmith, who traveled up and down the coast, perhaps trading new tools for old. We found tin oxide, the earliest yet found; blanks for bronze tools; whetstones; the ship's anvil; and a granite boulder. Much of the cargo was solidly stuck together by the thick layer of calcium carbonate sea growth that had formed over it. This simplified our drawing problem by allowing us to raise big pieces of cargo and sea growth together, pried loose by means of an ordinary hydraulic auto jack. These lumps could then be carefully excavated on the beach. When cleaned, they revealed heaps of copper ingots lying in the position into which they had fallen when the hull of the ship rotted away around them.

One of the most spectacular finds at Cape Gelidonya was part of the actual ship. When drawn, a direct comparison between it and the ship built by Ulysses, as described in the *Odyssey*, could be made. The last step in construction is filling the ship with brushwood, and scholars have puzzled for generations over the reason and meaning of this. Our wreck clearly showed that the brushwood had been put into the hull to protect the thin hull planking from the heavy cargo directly above it.

The archaeological conclusions that were made are many and varied. They can be summed up by saying that we proved that the wreck was that of a single ship, that we had fairly well established the origin of the cargo and the port where it was loaded. Our findings greatly contributed to the history of the movements of the Aegean Sea peoples at the beginning of European history. None of the objects we raised was of much intrinsic value; a large part of the value of the work lay in our being able to reconstruct partially, on paper, a trading ship of c. 1200 B.C. and its last voyage.

It had been variously proposed that underwater archaeology was impossible because "nothing much could be preserved underwater," or because "it is impossible to make proper plans underwater," or because "the work is too dangerous and outrageously expensive for the amount of information to be gained." All these predictions were proved wrong. A remarkable portion of the ship's cargo was preserved in good condition. We made respectable, if not perfect, plans. Using standard Navy procedures, we worked four to six divers for two dives a day to ninety feet for a total of seventy minutes' working time per day, in a place where the current sometimes ran up to two and a half knots and where helmet divers could not work even on a calm day without risk of an accident. The whole job had cost under twenty-five thousand dollars.

The success of the Cape Gelidonya expedition was due to several factors. First, political circumstances in Turkey were such that it was possible to get a permit to work. Second, the wreck was so important that it was possible to raise the money; and, third, most important of all, we had a clear idea of what we were doing technically and how we were going to go about it. A major cost-saving innovation was that we did without a ship. Previous large expeditions had allocated three-quarters of their budget to the ship.

The magic ingredients of a successful expedition must therefore be: *a known wreck*, which contains the treasure one seeks, intrinsic or not; *a permit* to excavate; the *technical ability* to do so; and *money*. Of course all this is useless unless you can find your wreck—which is where so many explorers of the deep fall by the wayside.

The Vicar of Bray *at Yerba Buena cove, San Francisco, during the gold rush, November 1849. Between April 1, 1847, and April 1, 1848, only four vessels anchored at San Francisco. One year later, following President Polk's announcement of the discovery of gold, nearly eight hundred ships departed from East Coast ports for San Francisco. Many were abandoned when their crews deserted to the gold fields and, like the whaler* Niantic *(at left), were pulled ashore to serve as buildings. The* Vicar, *drying her sails, escaped to continue life as a Cape Horn trader until she was hulked in the Falklands in 1880, where she remains to this day. Marine artist John Stobart spent hundreds of hours doing the research that led to this painting. With the help of Karl Kortum, of the San Francisco Maritime Museum, his painting is an accurate depiction of the scene.*

Preceding pages: *Lifting balloons at Cape Gelidonya and at Torre Sgaratta.*

Left: *A twelfth-century-A.D. Byzantine ship at Pelagos. A basketful of graffito-ware plates from the wreck arrives on board. After cleaning, handsome decorations were revealed: mythological beasts.*

37

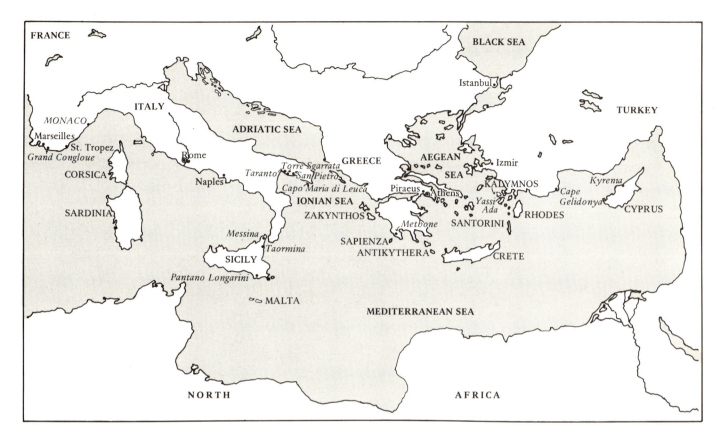

Preceding pages. Left: *The greatest undersea art treasure ever found is the archaic Poseidon or Zeus of Artemisium, now in the National Museum of Athens. The life-size bronze was discovered in 1927 by a sponge diver who was clearing a trawler's net.* Top right: *Part of the classical cargo from a wreck found off Lipari, Italy. The wreck is nearly three hundred feet down, far beyond practical diving range. Two German divers were killed in the 1969 expedition that recovered these bowls and candlesticks. The site was again explored in 1969 by the American Institute of Nautical Archaeology, using advanced deep diving techniques.* Bottom right: *The "Bishop's Cross," set with seven emeralds, was found by Teddy Tucker in one of three sixteenth-century Spanish wrecks he discovered off Bermuda in 1955. The cross—its back is removable—is probably the most valuable single find to come from North American waters.*

Students learn to sail Stormie Seas.

The first excavation of an ancient ship, carried out according to the established rules of modern land archaeology, was at Cape Gelidonya in 1960. The project was directed by George Bass and the author, under the auspices of the University of Pennsylvania Museum.

A camp was established on a beach an hour's sail from the wreck site and included, among other things, a portable photographic darkroom and a drawing office. The wreck itself was completely covered with three thousand three hundred years of sea growth. In the photograph above right, a diver wields a sledge hammer to free a block of concreted artifacts. The main cargo of the ship consisted of copper ingots that had been cast in Cyprus in about 1300 B.C. After they had been cleaned, the ingots were loaded onto a boat for the trip up the coast to the Bodrum Museum.

Some of the cargo consisted of bronze tools carried in rush baskets. The bottom of one of the baskets survived intact because it was caught between two copper ingots (the chemical action of the copper in the sea prevented marine animals from destroying it). Analysis of the reeds showed that the baskets had been made near Ras Shamra, Syria. The tools included pickaxes and various parts of them. Also found was the mouth of a Bronze Age stirrup jar.

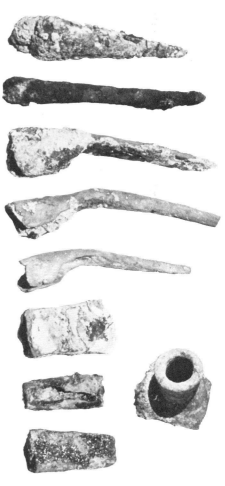

43

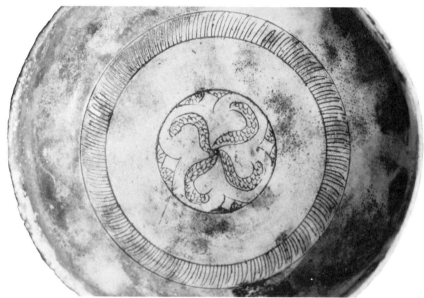
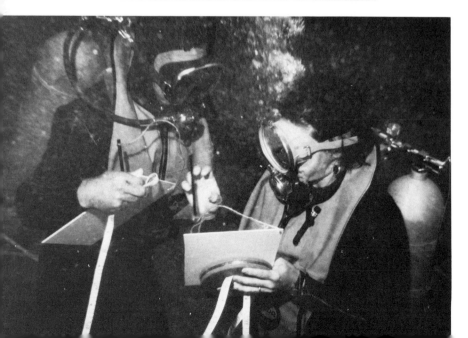

A large Byzantine ship carrying a cargo of amphorae and graffito-ware plates made somewhere near Constantinople sank near the island of Pelagos at the end of the twelfth century A.D. In 1970, our group surveyed the site for the Greek Archaeological Service.

One hundred and ten feet down, the sea bottom was covered with beautiful plates—they had been protected by a layer of silt and looked like new. Left: Draftsman and architect exchange notes on the bottom. Their slates are made of a plastic material that can be written on with an ordinary pencil and erased with kitchen cleanser.

Joan Throckmorton records the amphorae, a small part of the fifteen hundred finds raised from the wreck in two months.

The Wrecks and Their Whereabouts

A few years ago I stunned the distinguished audience at a seminar on "Science and Undersea Archaeology" when, after having been introduced as the man who had discovered more shipwrecks than anyone else present, I announced that, before beginning to explore the whereabouts of a wreck, the most necessary bit of equipment to have handy is a hangover pill. Hangover pills, I explained, were needed to cure the effects of long, boozy interviews with divers. Long, boozy interviews with divers? The reasoning behind this is quite simple: the best way to find wrecks is to talk to the people who have seen them.

Actually, most wrecks don't look like wrecks at all, or, at least, they scarcely fit the preconceptions of most people. And it follows that most people who have seen wrecks don't really know what they have seen. I am sure my own success in locating shipwrecks is due in large part to my training as a cultural anthropologist; local gossip and the ability to understand and analyze it is the key to most wreck finding. I imagine that the techniques employed by Margaret Mead in questioning Samoans about their sex lives were similar to my struggles with the sponge divers off southern Turkey. It's mostly a matter of asking the right questions, picking out the pertinent replies, and assembling your conclusions.

Quite naturally, and without realizing the significance of what they are doing, trawlers hang their nets on cannons (from the *Bonhomme Richard*) or ancient statues (from the Artemisium wreck) or over heaps of ancient amphorae. Sponge divers stumble across ancient anchors. Northern sports divers hunt lobsters in the shattered timbers of what may have been a barge or a clipper ship or a Royal Navy frigate or a Spanish galleon.

Since the introduction of helmet diving gear in the latter part of the nineteenth century, Aegean sponge divers have spent more time on the bottom of the sea than anyone else in the world. They know the ocean floor as a farmer knows his field, and will sometimes show sites to people they like or trust. Patience, a certain amount of linguistic skill, and a strong head and stomach for whatever is served in the local cafés have matched and even surpassed scientific magic boxes in the number of wrecks found. One day soon, as further technological progress is made, the balance may swing the other way.

During the summers of 1958 and 1959 I undertook a survey of the Turkish Aegean which resulted in the discovery of the wreck of the Gelidonya ship and dozens of other shipwrecks, including several at Yassi Ada that have been excavated by the University of Pennsylvania Museum. The success of the projects can be largely attributed to the friendly cooperation of the sponge divers of Bodrum, especially Captain Kemal Arras, who showed us many of the sites he had found in his years of searching the sea bottom for sponges. In fact, most of our exploratory diving was done from Captain Kemal's thirty-six-foot sponge boat *Mandalinci* during the course of his normal sponge-diving activities.

There is a tenuous borderline between known and unknown wrecks. They come in two categories. First there are those that can be found at historical battle sites—sites that are more or less definitely known. For instance, we know that the battle of Navarino was fought in Greece in 1827. Rumors of gold aboard the flagship of the Turkish fleet led to a salvage attempt in the early 1900s. Helmet divers found the ship one hundred and seventy-five feet down, with her upper works protruding from the mud. But as the upper works were so shaky, the divers would not risk entering the ship and instead dynamited the hull and dragged the timbers into shallow water, where some are still visible.

Another example is the site of the battle of

Salamis, waged between Persians and Athenians. No one has ever found any remains, but no one has ever looked very seriously. The triremes may have swamped rather than sunk, but there must be some scraps of the big and protracted collision between the two great powers. The water is deep, however, and the site has become a nonstop shipping lane ever since, and indeed was one long before the battle took place. The tonnage in tin cans alone must be enough to provoke a magnetometer to blow its mind!

Sometimes individual ships are known to have sunk on a given historical occasion. The *Vasa*, a Swedish warship sunk in Stockholm harbor, is one. Now raised, it is being preserved as a wonderful museum. The *Mary Rose*, sunk near Portsmouth in the fifteenth century, is another. Alexander McKee searched on and off for years and found her—no mean accomplishment in the dark waters of a major shipping lane.

The second category of known-unknown wrecks are those that simply occur in likely places. A reef just under the surface in a much-used channel has certainly accounted for the loss of some number, great or small, of sailing ships. Yassi Ada, near ancient Halicarnassus (modern Bodrum) in Turkey, is one, and the southern coast of Italy between Taranto and Capo Santa Maria di Leuca is another. There is no safe harbor of any size in the whole stretch of this Italian shoreline, and in the course of several summers we surveyed half a dozen wrecks, dived on a number of others, and heard of still more. A ship caught in a strong southerly gale, unable to anchor in deep water, or unsatisfactorily anchored in shallow water, had no place to go but aground once she could not or was afraid to plunge safely out into the open sea.

Similarly, the coasts of Florida and Texas are traps for sailing ships caught in the seasonal hurricanes of the region. The relatively clumsy square-riggers of the Spanish fleets with cargoes of silver and gold that set out from Vera Cruz in the sixteenth and seventeenth centuries inevitably drove onto the shore when caught in such foul weather. It happened in 1554, when at least a dozen ships drove onto Padre Island; several more might have ended up as far away as Florida. The 1715 hurricane destroyed another such fleet, part of which was discovered and salvaged by Kip Wagner, a retired house carpenter.

There are wrecks everywhere in the world that ships have sailed. Finding the unrecorded ones means having an intimate knowledge of wind, weather, and currents, and of the decisions that sailing shipmasters must make. Our little research vessel *Stormie Seas* is properly rigged and sails well. Yet, in the six years I have sailed her all around the eastern Mediterrean. I have on several occasions found myself in situations that could have been fatal to a vessel of her type if she had been mismanaged, just plain unlucky, or if her engine had given way. In nearly every one of these hazardous situations an exploratory dive proved that an ancient shipmaster, either unlucky or mistaken in his judgment, had wrecked his ship in precisely the spots where I myself had escaped.

Before a discussion of search techniques, some mention should be made of what we can hope to look for. To date, the most interesting wrecks are likely to be the most difficult to find—that is, those completely covered by mud and sand, or in very deep water. Presently we depend on those with some remnants showing on the surface of the bottom, in divable depths.

The only useful approach to this problem is a study of the various kinds of wrecks. If a ship goes down onto rocky bottom in shallow water, she breaks up very quickly. Pieces of her can be scattered for miles. If she happens to sink in deep water onto sand bottom, she will settle into the bottom and parts of her will be preserved.

Teredos, or shipworms, have always been a prob-

At the Great Basses Reef, Sri Lanka. Mike Wilson examines the anchor (above) that belonged to a British merchantman lost here some time before the Crimean War. Right, top to bottom: Another wreck, found nearby, was a 22-gun ship of unknown nationality that went ashore in 1704. Her cargo consisted of silver coins from Surat, which had been minted by Aurangzeb, the Mogul Emperor whose father, Shah Jahan, built the Taj Mahal. Mike inspects the "Silver Gulch," an area packed full of the silver rupees that had been shipped one thousand to each coconut-fiber sack. The sacks lasted long enough for

the fast-growing coral to cement their contents together. A bronze one-pounder gun survived in perfect condition, even to the shot and powder in the barrel and the teakwood tampion that covered the muzzle.

lem for saltwater mariners, especially in warm seas like the Mediterranean. The sunken wreck of a wooden ship will be seriously weakened by teredos within three years, riddled in five, and almost destroyed in less than twenty. If the wreck lies in less than about seventy-five feet of water, it can be broken up and scattered by wave action as soon as it loses its structural strength. The deeper a wreck lies, the better preserved it is likely to be. Some parts of the Mediterranean floors are covered with a deep layer of soft sedimentary ooze, and wrecks that have fallen into this layer must be preserved almost intact.

Albert Falco spotted a remarkable example of this while surveying from Cousteau's famous submarine *Souçoupe* for an oil pipeline across the Strait of Gibraltar. There, a thousand feet down, was a group of amphorae, standing upright just as they had been stacked into the hold of a forgotten Roman ship two thousand years ago. The ship itself had disappeared, leaving the amphorae in the same position in which they had been loaded. This can have occurred only if the rate of disintegration of the wood at that depth had been much slower than at, say, three hundred feet, which gave the coralline limestone sea growth and shells, which form on pottery or stone, time enough to develop and hold the stack together before it lost the support of the wooden structure around it. I encountered a similar case off Ceylon, when Arthur Clarke and I were working on the 1703–1704 Great Basses wreck. Silver coins had been shipped in coconut fiber sacks. Coir (coconut fiber) is very resistant to rot and attack by marine animals. It lasted long enough for the coins in the sacks to be solidly concreted together: consequently, we found lumps of coins in the shape of sacks.

It is difficult to estimate the exact time it would take any given wreck to be destroyed, because of the several factors involved that can never be constant: size of timbers, kind of wood, rate of sediment deposit, rate of limestone sea-growth deposit, and frequency of teredos and other destructive marine organisms in the area where the wreck lies.

Modern wrecks and their rate of disintegration are good guides to the possible condition of ancient wrecks in similar locations. The eventual preservation of a ship and its cargo depends on what happens to the wreck in the first few years after sinking. If parts of the hull, and organic material preserved within the hull, survive the first fifty years underwater, they will probably last thousands more.

In recent years more than eighty wrecks of ships dating from the fourteenth century to the early nineteenth have been found in Holland, in areas where land has been reclaimed from the sea. These ships sank onto a soft mud bottom in shallow water. The upper parts of the hulls soon rotted and washed away, leaving the bottoms, which had been rapidly filled with mud, preserved intact. In some cases the sides had collapsed outward, to be covered in turn by the protecting mud. Very few objects were found from the upper parts of these ships, which had been scattered by wave action as the wreck was breaking up.

A wreck in deep water just collapses slowly into the mud. If the wreck is in an area where there is a mild current that can build up sediment inside it, and if the wreck lies on its side, it can conceivably be filled up within a few years and be preserved. Under normal conditions the uppermost part of the wreck will be destroyed, or will be found collapsed, unless the buildup of sediment is very rapid.

The great problem, again, is that well-preserved wrecks are hard to find. With the methods available to us at this point, we can have only a chance of finding those ships that carried bulky, imperishable cargoes, now protruding from the bottom to mark the spot. Ancient wrecks found in the Aegean and elsewhere preserve most of the bottom of the ship under

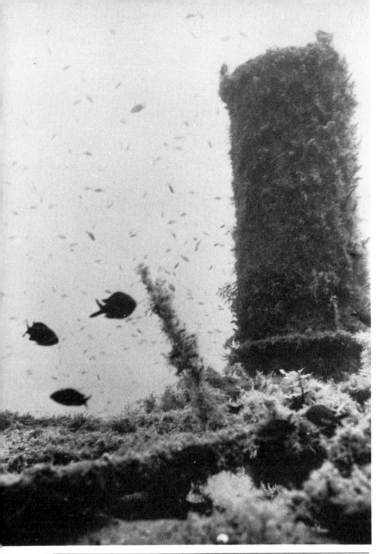

Previous page: *A diver enters the galley of the S.S. Artemis, a vessel that was sunk in 1942 by allied torpedo planes in the harbor of Milos, Greece, while she awaited a convoy to take her cargo of ammunition to Rommel's Africa Corps. Today she lies in one hundred and eighty feet of water, intact and almost untouched: her dangerous cargo makes her impossible to salvage.*

A ghost ship on a voyage to nowhere. Artemis's cargo booms are still rigged (above, right). After twenty-five years her wooden parts have mostly disappeared, and shipworms have reduced the diameter of her topmast, which was originally the same size as the steel lower mast (above). The bones of her engineer lie on top of the low-pressure cylinder of the big triple-expansion steam engine (right). It is expected that she will stand as a structure for perhaps another fifty years before she collapses into a heap of junk on the seabed.

the turn of the bilge. Ships that carried heavy deck cargoes sometimes have parts of their decks intact. If a ship's cargo shifted as she went to the bottom and she took a heavy list, we could hope to find one side of the ship intact, from bulwark to keel.

Once a more or less specific location is known or suspected, one must then actually find the wreck, which is where the real work begins. In the least complicated of circumstances, ancient Uncle X arranges, for example, to take the searcher out on his trawler to the site of a wreck he or his diver nephew or his dead grandfather knew like the nose on his mother's face. Whole days, indeed months, can pass in the search, since fine navigation is the worst of problems the searcher for wrecks has to face.

If a smallish general area is known, several different search methods may be used. Swimmers can fan out and circle or square-sweep the area, spacing themselves along a line at intervals appropriate to circumstances of visibility. Divers can do the same. In England this has been done very effectively in searching for Armada shipwrecks. Obviously depths where any noticeable decompression time is involved are less salutary for this sort of search than shallow water where time is limited only by those problems that do not have to do with depth.

Such a search by divers, assuming part of the wreck lies on the surface of the bottom, is probably as good as one can get at the moment. (Assuming also that the wreck lies in presently practicable diving depths—a formidable pair of assumptions.) Submersibles of many sorts are working now, have been used for some time, and are continually undergoing improvement. The aim of all of them, whether manned or directed from the surface, is to provide for vision, careful navigation, and, in some cases, lift, with more or less delicacy, without exposing divers to the danger of decompression sickness, without the expense and sometimes hazard of diving on mixed gases, and without the waste of mental efficiency that occurs with the most experienced of divers somewhere near a hundred feet and increases rapidly with depth.

Here a qualification must be made—finicky on paper, but of considerable importance in practice. The sweep-by-divers method of search is effective exactly in proportion to how much individual divers can *see*. Masts protruding show a new wreck, parts of the hull an older one, but, generally, with an old wreck there are only heaps of pottery, ballast stones, or heavily overgrown cannon showing, and these may be nearly indistinguishable from the surrounding seascape.

Underwater archaeology is a very new quasi-science, and few people indeed have done anything approximating the practice in the field that would be required of a physician in order to remove a patient's tonsils. And some of these people have better natural eyes than others for telling the difference between a bit of broken pot covered with sea growth and a bit of rock covered with sea growth. Talent is something; experience is a lot. Both are in comparatively short supply, all things considered.

Two examples: There is only one Frederic Dumas, who has been diving and looking for wrecks during much of his adult life. He can home like a pigeon for a wreck site where most divers would see only a continuing expanse of seascape, one bit much like the next—rocks, sand, mud, dubious lumps, all ornamented confusingly with a profusion of primitive sea creatures, plants, and animals indistinguishable from one another much of the time.

Here your single-profession professional runs into trouble. Underwater expeditions are often plagued by and sometimes rescued by "the most experienced salvage diver in the . . ." and "the most gifted student my department has trained for . . ." and "this superb photographer who jumped the . . ." Some of these VIP's can see, and some can't. Terry Vose, an

American who couldn't dive and had no training in archaeology at all, came along one summer and offered to help out in the engine room for a day or two. One thing led to another, Terry learned to dive, and during the years we worked together he proved to have a first-class eye, ashore as well as under the sea, for distinguishing natural objects from those made by man.

If the area is too deep or too big for search by people, we must turn to instruments. Perhaps we will soon be able to rely solely on technology, but not yet. Everyone in the field is concerned with the vast consumption of manpower for comparatively small returns.

Dr. Harold Edgerton, professor emeritus of electrical engineering at the Massachusetts Institute of Technology, has pioneered with sonar, learning how sound waves, striking and penetrating the bottom, can return a description of the sea floor in the form of graphs that can be interpreted by a skilled reader. A second device, the side-scan sonar, "sees" anomalies at a considerable distance on either side of its own path over the sea.

Recently in Porto Longo, a small harbor on Sapienza, an island off the southern coast of mainland Greece, Dr. Edgerton spent considerable time surveying the whole harbor, finding many anomalies, on the larger of which divers then dug with an airlift. The sonar recorded several wrecks that were known to be there (a couple were visible from the surface on a clear day), and found several more piles of ballast. It could not, curiously, manage to notice a large wooden wreck that lies in plain sight.

Later, in the same harbor, Dr. E. T. Hall used a proton magnetometer in a similar survey. The magnetometer recorded some of the same sites as the sonar and noted several others. These sites have not yet been explored by divers. Again, there were known sites which the magnetometer could not find.

One of the worst problems in finding wrecks and returning to them, once found, is navigation. Getting from England to France is one thing—eventually, one is bound to bump into the other shore. But locating a small site at any distance from shore, handling a ship on a less than calm sea with a dim coastline for reference, can be a terrible problem.

Porto Longo is a little harbor, a mile or so at its longest, very much less than in width, and even there we had many difficulties, in spite of first having done a complete land survey of the entire harbor. Numbered marks were painted at close intervals right around the harbor, those on the east side lining up with those on the west. Even so, running the sonar back and forth over these east-west tracks by dinghy produced a lot of trouble, as we found in trying to return to sonar signals to buoy them. Slight changes in wind, otherwise unnoticeable current, difficulties in seeing the white paint and flags on the marks all showed that the system needed improvement.

Later, with Dr. Hall's magnetometer survey, this problem was solved by having someone on shore, with radio and transit, direct the boat on its track. The magnetometer survey party felt that they were seldom, if ever, more than a meter off course.

The lesson we learned from the Porto Longo experience was simply that it was very easy to collect masses of data with electronic instruments, but hardly as easy to interpret the data efficiently unless one had a superior navigational system.

Dr. Edgerton and I went on from Porto Longo to search for the Turkish ships lost in the Gulf of Lepanto in 1571. After months of side-scan sonar searches we discovered an anomaly that was the right size and shape for what might be left of the ship's galleys. We ran a magnetometer over the site, and its readings confirmed our estimate. Several years later Dr. Edgerton found the *Monitor,* and in 1976 Sidney Wignall found what is almost certainly the wreck of the *Bonhomme Richard*. Both Dr. Edgerton and Sid Wignall used essentially the same methods as the Gulf of Lepanto search.

The most incredible sonar record I have seen was produced in the fall of 1975 by a dedicated group of Canadians, led by Dr. Daniel Nelson, a dentist and amateur marine archaeologist from St. Catharines, Ontario, and sponsored by the Royal Ontario Museum. With a good bit of historical research under their belt, they were able to establish that the American-armed schooners the *Hamilton* and the *Scourge* had foundered somewhere to the west of the mouth of the Niagara River in August 1812. They began to search, using a Klein Hydroscan side-scan sonar and data recording system developed by Martin Klein, a former student of Dr. Edgerton, who was a veteran of sonar searches in the Mediterranean.

After four years of search the awesome result was a perfect sonar picture of one of the schooners, with masts, bowsprit, and jibboom still in place. It lay in three hundred feet of water, fifteen miles west of the mouth of the Niagara River—preserved, presumably forever, by the icy cold, almost anaerobic waters of Lake Ontario.

It follows, then, that given the right geological conditions—a smooth, sandy, or muddy bottom and sufficient depth—almost any known wreck can be found within several feet by the right combination of side-scanning sonar, magnetometer, and sophisticated navigational systems.

In addition, the searcher must have a vast knowledge of what is likely to survive from a given period, the sea itself, and the people who work there. At this writing, the most recent important discoveries have been the wrecks of the *Monitor*, the *Bonhomme Richard*, and that at Dhokos, Greece. The first two were found with sophisticated electronics and a pairing of good historical research and good seamanship. The *Monitor*'s records were known; thus the technical problem of finding her was the straightforward one of sweeping with side-scanning sonar the area where she was known to be, identifying and locating all anomalies, analyzing each one, then photographing the most likely candidates. The *Bonhomme Richard* was found in much the same way, with the search precipitated some years back by the find of a cannon of the right type and date.

The earliest shipwreck yet found, the early Bronze Age ship off Dhokos, was discovered by simple swim searches, with no special equipment at all, except for mask and fins and an educated eye for pottery.

The Dhokos find came about through an interesting set of political circumstances. In the summer of 1975 our groups had planned to survey a series of ancient wrecks off Greece on behalf of the Hellenic Institute of Marine Archaeology, of which I was then technical director. I obtained funds for ship time and acquired a crew of old hands from other expeditions: Jim Löfstrand, a mathematician, skipper, and oceanographer; Lesley Whale and Fred Yalouris, archaeologist; Victoria Jennsen, a conservator; and Peter Nicholaides, a diving physiologist. When crew and equipment had been assembled, the Greek authorities forbade us to dive with mechanical equipment, even though local commercial divers were taking tourists out with aqualungs. We decided to hold a seminar on the relationship between ancient and modern people and the ecosystem of the Gulf of Hydra. The group skin dived every likely cape in the Gulf, in order to study remains of ancient occupation in the form of pottery fallen from the shore, land evidence of human occupation, and the ecology of the sea itself.

In the course of this survey we saw dozens of broken-up ancient shipwrecks, nearly all late Roman or Byzantine. The Dhokos wreck looked like all the others, except that it was thousands of years older. It would never have been identified if Jennson, Whale,

Searching for shipwrecks with sonar. Top left: Stormie Seas *in the Gulf of Lepanto, with sonar boom rigged.* Bottom left: *Schematic drawing shows how sound waves emanate from a side-scan sonar "fish."* Top right: *A World War II steel ship at the bottom of the Gulf of Lepanto, as seen by Harold Edgerton's side-scanning sonar.* Bottom right: *A side-scan sonar image of either the* Scourge *or the* Hamilton, *both American Navy armed schooners sunk in Lake Ontario in 1812. Note that topmasts and bowsprit are still in place. The wrecks are over three hundred feet down and have been preserved intact by the chilly water at the bottom of the lake.*

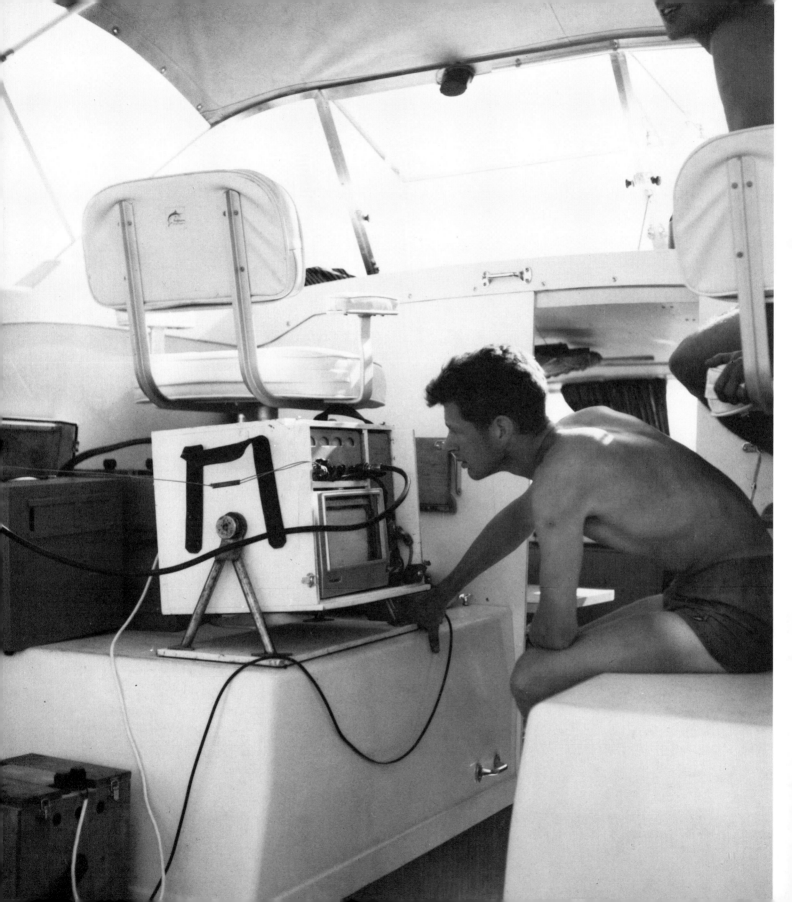

Opposite: *A crew member watches the proton magnetometer.* Top left: *Professor Harold Edgerton (standing) of the Massachusetts Institute of Technology and the author with a prototype side-scan sonar "fish."* Bottom left: *Side-scan sonar recorder (foreground) and "fish" about to go over the stern.*

and I had not been lecturing the others on the standard field archaeological problem of recognizing broken pots.

Dhokos fizzled for political reasons. It is hoped that the project will be continued and that George Bass will be persuaded to repeat his Bronze Age triumph of Cape Gelidonya.

With the help of the Admiralty Library and the Public Records Office, I have located most of the known Royal Navy wrecks in the eastern Mediterranean. The ones that I never got to were located by that indefatigable treasure hunter and researcher of Spanish Armada fame, Robert Stenuit. One was H.M.S. *Athénienne,* lost with more than four hundred men on the Skerki rocks, between Sicily and Tunisia. Robert Stenuit's attention was drawn to the *Athénienne* by a reference to ten thousand pounds in "specie" —silver—on board. He found the court-martial documents, found what was left of the wreck, and found the silver—alas, the silver had turned to worthless silver sulfate! Luckily I met him and heard his account before I wasted time and money in a parallel search.

Working with public records can, sometimes, backfire. A few years ago a well-known undersea explorer, who is neither a scholar nor an archaeologist, spent months and hundreds of thousands of dollars searching for the right wreck on the wrong reef. He did not know that the area's name had changed since the seventeenth century. Working with archives is very much like working with computer data; the

right questions have to be asked before the archives can be expected to provide the right answers.

Eighteenth-century wrecks, like that of H.M.S. *Nautilus,* discovered on the Nautilus rocks in the Aegean, are interesting because of their historical associations Scholars should work on them because, with the advent of skin diving as a sport, such remnants will disappear completely in the very near future. Using the eighteenth- and early-nineteenth-century archives of the Royal Navy in order to find wrecks is a fascinating study in itself. In the case of the *Nautilus,* we found the court-martial documents of the surviving officers and men of the ship, and when we visited the site we were able to re-create vividly in our minds that night in January 1807 when the *Nautilus,* driving at nine knots under reefed topsails with the north wind behind her, smashed on a corner of Nautilus rock and within ten minutes became a total wreck.

The *Nautilus* incident brings us back to Nelson's

Dhokos: the site of the oldest shipwreck in the world. The ship had probably been moored at approximately the spot where the Greek yacht is anchored, and then blown onto the rocks to the boat's right. Plentiful remains of a settlement that seems to date from about 2400 to 1200 B.C. are scattered over the area to the boat's left.

Top: *Pottery from the wreck included a typical early Bronze Age askos, an amphora handle, and the spouts of pitchers.* Bottom: *The wreck appeared as a mass of broken pottery, mixed with stones. The diver, equipped only with breathing tube, fins, and mask, began to feel the pressure of the sixty-foot depth he had reached.*

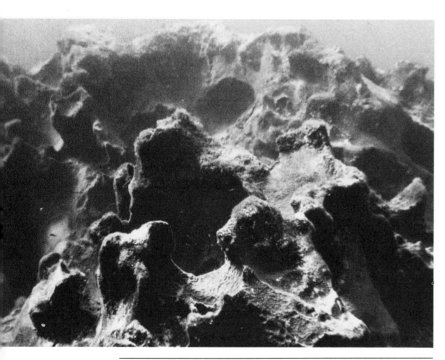

The wreck of HMS Nautilus at Nautilus rocks, which she struck in 1807. Her cannon (top left) has lost its trunnions because of the giant seas that pound this reef during most of the year. Right: Turkish copper coins from the wreck of the British frigate Cambrian, lost at Grambousa, Crete, in 1828. Coins were probably petty cash for local purchases.

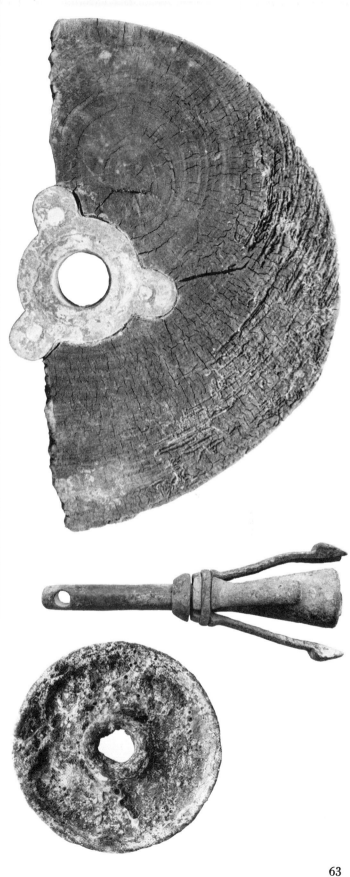

Joan Throckmorton with straps of a pulley block from the Cambrian.

A bronze tool for cleaning a cannon (center right), stamped with the broad arrow of the Royal Navy, was evidence that we had found the Cambrian. *Lignum vitae sheaves (top right) and hundreds of bronze sheaves (below right) were also among the finds. The wooden structure of this huge ship has completely disappeared.*

navy, and to Admiral Collingwood, who was destined never to receive the dispatches that the *Nautilus* was carrying to him.

Nothing of the ship herself remains. No matter; we have her plans. A silver spoon that we discovered in the heap of ballast bars, which is all that remains, was identified as having belonged to the captain. If wrecks of this kind are forgotten, the small objects that remain will soon disappear into the hands of skin divers, where they have a good chance of being lost or of disintegrating completely through lack of conservation. Although no great historical problems can be resolved by such investigations, it is my belief that the scattered souvenirs of this dramatic and fascinating period of naval history should be preserved in museums, where everybody can see them.

Another Royal Navy vessel found from her records was H.M.S. *Cambrian*, which ran aground off Crete while bombarding pirates in 1828. My diving partner, Alekos Papadongonas, then Greek Navy Commander, and I were both fascinated by the role that the *Cambrian* had filled during the Greek Revolution, when her captain, Gowan Edwin Hamilton, had acted as a kind of umpire, reconciling the differences between disgruntled Englishmen who had been robbed by Greek privateers, the Greek Government, His Majesty's Government, and the French. Hamilton was one of the unsung heroes of the Greek Revolution and architect of the Anglo-Greek "special relationship" which survives to this day. Our aim was to attempt to understand Hamilton and the wreck of the *Cambrian*. There was no real treasure to be found; the *Cambrian*'s only valuable cargo had been the long-delayed watercolors of the Parthenon, executed by Lusieri for Lord Elgin a generation before the wreck. Armed with the photostats of the court-martial documents, we set forth and found the wreck on the first dive.

Both the *Nautilus* and the *Cambrian* cannon and ballast bars had been taken by Greek sponge divers. What remained to mark the graves were a few cannonballs, lots of broken pottery, and, in the case of the *Cambrian*, thousands of Turkish copper coins.

With the exception of Dhokos and the Royal Navy wrecks, nearly all the undocumented wrecks I have found have been products of my own specialized knowledge of sponge divers and their world, and an ability to make meaningful an inarticulate Greek or Turkish diver's description of an underwater site.

In foreign regions of the world the sea searcher must begin with an anthropologist's understanding of the area and the people who inhabit it. Generally, this means familiarizing oneself with the language. In the Mediterranean, for instance, one must have a good ear for the sea dialects of fishermen and sponge divers.

The profession of the sponge diver is dying. Today the young men of the Greek sponge-diving islands have mostly opted for normal seagoing, which pays better and is less dangerous. The few surviving Greek sponge boats are often manned by Turks from the villages of Lycia and Caria, during periods when relations between the two countries permit. Yet old traditions die hard in traditional places, and something still survives.

Top, left: *Sponge divers dragging a grapnel in order to locate a reef. Their equipment is identical to that used by the divers who worked the* Mentor *in 1803. The only improvement: an inboard motor!* Left: *The entrance to St. Nicholas Bay, where the British merchant brig* Mentor, *carrying marbles from the Parthenon, struck and sank in September 1802. The actual wreck site is at the far right of the photograph in sixty feet of water.*

The Divers

Except for the waterfront on the island of Kalymnos, the best place to meet sponge divers in Greece is a café in Piraeus called the Navarinon. Nothing distinguishes it from a dozen or so others on the Akti Miaouli, the main street of Piraeus; they are all large rooms where ordinary-looking men sit at marble-topped tables, drink coffee, smoke one another's cigarettes, and talk.

This is the seamen's headquarters for all Greece, not only for the mainland sailors who man the steel ships of the modern Greek merchant marine, but also for the islanders who sail small wooden ships around the Aegean. These sponge boatmen from Limnos, Tricheri, Aegina, Skiathos, Symē, and, most of all, Kalymnos, sit in the rear left-hand corner of the café and talk business. In the morning they discuss sponge prices, problems of dealing with the government of North Africa, the latest situation with the Turks, engines and boats, who plans to work where this year or next. At lunchtime they disappear but return sometime after five. Then the older men come in, those who tend to drink ouzo instead of coffee, and if the listener is in luck, he will hear one them begin a story, full of wonder: "It was in the month of April, April was the month . . . ," and on into a tale of that other world the old man visited several times a day for forty years and now, retired, remember with both satisfaction and regret.

That drab corner has heard sagas worthy of a new Odyssey, of clever men in little ships exploring strange corners of the Mediterranean or the Florida Keys, of dynamite and shipwrecks, contraband rifles, bouts with piracy, agony, death, pride, money, and gold—black gold growing there, in that other world, waiting for brave men to come and take it. For these men the pursuit of sponges provides them with romance and high adventure. The tale that rates rapt attention from everybody is one that recounts the day Nikos found enough sponges to fill the foredeck of his small ship, or the other, in 1926, when Captain Christos found a virgin bank containing enough sponges to pay back the advances on his journey and buy a new boat. The world of the sponge diver is old and different and strange, and, like the sponges they collect, the divers do not quite fit into the contemporary world of chrome and plastic.

In 1976 there were only about three hundred divers—all islanders, mostly Kalymnians—left. Once there were thousands, but now Kalymnos is the only island with a sponge fleet. The harbors of Symē, Aegina, and Hydra, which rivaled Kalymnos at the turn of the century, are today almost empty of sponge boats. Smaller sponge centers from the old days, such as Limnos, Tricheri, and Skiathos, still have a tradition of diving, but it is rapidly dying. In 1949, the first year that the waters off Africa were opened to divers after the war, two hundred and twenty-nine boats were fitted out in Greece. Today there are only about thirty working sponge boats.

Out of this number only half a dozen still practice traditional naked diving, which has almost disappeared after a history that can be traced to very ancient times. Symē, always an island of sponge divers, is said to have been founded by Glaucus, the legendary diver who accompanied the Argonauts. Naked-diving methods cannot have changed very much from ancient times. Divers work from a small boat, which is rowed along until the captain, positioned in the bows, spots a sponge. He then extends a long pole or a weight on a line down to it, and sends the diver down the same path. In ancient times the captain dropped a bit of olive oil onto the sea, making a clear window on the smooth surface of the water. Today he looks through a glass-bottom bucket.

Fishermen at Methone clean their gill nets.

The key to success is the captain's sharp eye, for it is difficult to see sponges underwater. The valuable commercial sponge hides under rocks, in crevices, or behind weeds. The worthless "wild" sponge grows, perversely, in the open. There are a hundred wild sponges for each valuable one. A man with a keen eye can sense sponges, detecting their presence by scanning the spot where they ought to be.

Where the water became too deep for poles or weights, the captain sent the naked diver down with a flat marble stone, about three inches thick and oblong in shape, and thirty pounds in weight. The diver breathed deeply many times to build up a reserve of oxygen, then leaped, headfirst, letting the stone drag him toward rocks that the captain thought "smelled" spongy. On reaching the bottom, he dropped the stone, picked sponges for about half a minute, and was then snatched to the surface by a line attached both to him and to the stone. This line was cleverly tied so that, if the stone got stuck on the bottom, the diver could not be trapped.

Many stories are told about the prowess of these naked divers. The gist of them is that a first-rate naked diver could go down more than one hundred and eighty feet. There is one reliable account of a naked sponge diver descending to two hundred and six feet to recover a warship's anchor.

A few years ago a friend and I experimented with this type of diving, except that we added a mask and fins. With the flat stones acting as an aquaplane, we were able to go down more than one hundred feet without much trouble, and we felt we could have gone deeper with practice. This kind of diving is exhilarating.

It was easy to understand why the naked divers had always used a rope. Although a naked diver is normally buoyant because of the air in his lungs, air was so compressed after sixty feet that our buoyancy was negative and we tended, disconcertingly, to sink.

A second hazard is anoxia. A diver can lose consciousness without warning when the oxygen in his lungs is used up. If this occurs he must be immediately pulled to the surface. Although too much oxygen deprivation can cause brain damage, he will usually be unharmed.

A history of the naked divers of Kalymnos and Symē has never been written, but the occasional references to them are fascinating. The ancient references are mostly lost, including *The Diver* by Kroton; *Glafkos the Sailor*, a tragedy by Aeschylus; and a comedy by Menander. Kointos of Smyrna speaks in the fifth century B.C. of the men of Symē as the best sponge fishers. When the brig *Mentor* was wrecked off Kythēra, her cargo of the Elgin marbles was salvaged from sixty feet of water by divers from Symē. Some thirty years later, Kalymnian divers were salvaging cannon from the sunken Turkish fleet at Navarino.

The pattern of diving in the Mediterranean was radically changed for the first time in the early nineteenth century, when naked divers from Symē and Kalymnos began to go to Africa in great numbers, followed by divers from other diving islands. The big change occurred in the 1860s when the divers of Symē began to work with modern helmet diving gear. It's told that the men of Symē refused to use the cumbersome gear until the wife of the captain who had brought it from Europe dived in it herself. She shamed the doubters.

A glance at a helmet suit explains their reluctance. Constructed as if expressly to produce claustrophobia, it is a heavy rubberized twill suit into which the diver is helped through a rubber ring around the wide neck. His hands are shoved through tight cuffs with the aid of soft soap and soon begin to turn blue as blood circulation slows. He then sits on the bench, and a bronze breastplate is fitted under the rubber ring and attached to it with large bronze wing nuts.

This cuts deeply into his collarbone, and, because it is so heavy, he cannot sit upright.

Next come two kidney-shaped lead weights, one in the small of the back, the other over his navel. Then someone runs a piece of rope from the back of the breastplate, between his legs, and up to the front of the breastplate, heaving so hard that the already cramped diver must stoop to avoid being bisected. Meanwhile, someone else has been putting on his shoes, weighted heavily with lead or iron. A bag for sponges is lashed to the breastplate. He is instructed to lean forward continually.

They clap the helmet over his head and push him overboard, where he proceeds to apply the principles of compressed-air diving in which he has been instructed. These are simple. In order to breathe underwater, a man's lungs must respond with pressure equal to that of the surrounding sea. To accomplish this, compressed air is fed from a compressor in the boat through a hose down to the diver, who literally uses his head to work a valve in the helmet which controls the inflow of air. The suit should be filled with air to below the level of the diver's lungs. Too much air will make the suit too buoyant, and the diver, out of control, will shoot to the surface. Too frequent use of the head valve will cause difficulty in breathing, as the pressure of the sea squeezes the suit around his body.

After a few dives, however, initial fear of the suit wears off and the diver learns to move around comfortably, though never as freely as he would with modern free-diving gear. He can remain underwater for many hours, in a world of cool blue and gray, with specks of colors never seen before and suspended laws of gravity and space.

For the helmet divers of Symē and Kalymnos this was the world at whose doors their ancestors had been battering since before history. Its floor was covered with money. The helmet diving gear had as dramatic an effect on the sponge diving island as the invention of the cotton gin on the American South. It brought gold in incredible amounts to the islands, especially Kalymnos and Symē, where captains, owners, and sponge merchants built huge stone houses and bought Parisian dresses for their daughters.

Their life was changed in still another way, for with riches the helmet rig brought terror. The effects of prolonged breathing of compressed air are not easy to explain to laymen even after a hundred years of study. At that time they were unimaginable. What occurs is that a diver, breathing compressed air at a considerable depth for a prolonged period, will absorb nitrogen gas into his body tissues. Unlike oxygen, which is absorbed, nitrogen gas must return to the bloodstream. If the diver returns slowly enough to the surface, the nitrogen is passed off harmlessly into the blood; if he rises too quickly, the tissues discharge this gas into the blood in the form of bubbles.

The result will be one of the various forms of caisson disease, or bends. If a bubble stops a heart valve, the diver has heart failure. If one gets into the blood vessels in the spinal cord, paralysis results. A common minor bend occurs in joints, such as the elbows or shoulders. This is not fatal, but it is excruciatingly painful. The only prevention is to limit the diver's time underwater and require an ascent slow enough to prevent the formation of these bubbles. The only cure is recompression.

None of this was understood when helmet gear was introduced in the Aegean. Once their initial reluctance had been overcome, the islanders took to the gear with immense enthusiasm, after a lifetime of hanging onto rocks and getting blurred glimpses of another world containing riches beyond their reach. They went deep, stayed down too long, and died. Half the men died the first season on the first helmet diving boat fitted out in Kalymnos. The women of the island banded together in a screaming mob to pronounce anathema on the dealer who had introduced the new gear.

By the end of the century the situation was so bad that Charles Flegel, an Austrian professor studying the sponge industry in the Dodecanese islands, spent the rest of his life campaigning against the use of helmet gear. He succeeded in getting the Sultan to forbid use of helmet gear in the Turkish empire, but this law was never enforced.

In 1907 the first decompression tables were published in Europe, stating the length of time a diver might safely remain at stated depths. But by then two generations of trial and error had left a trail of shallow graves on the shore from Tunisia to the Sea of Marmara, and sponge divers had developed their own system of diving. They worked consistently at depths far beyond those considered practical for naval and commercial divers.

As for the sponge-diving boat, it must be large enough for her crew to live and cook on board, yet readily maneuverable so it can stay over the diver when he is on the bottom. A sponge boat never anchors while working, but is led by the diver, who is attached to the boat by the umbilical cords of his air hose and lifeline.

The favorite boats for diving are called *aktarmades,* a variation of the *trechendiri* or standard double-ended fishing boat of the Aegean, apparently the descendant of a very ancient design. Like everything else having to do with sponge diving, the boat has been modified to fit the trade. *Aktarmades* are fuller and have higher bows than the ordinary *trechendiria,* the most common Greek sailing ships; they are seldom less than thirty feet long or more than forty-five.

In these boats men can stay at sea for months at a time. Their social organization, probably as old as sponge diving, has been modified to fit the new helmet gear. The captain, as one would expect, commands. He is responsible for the divers and may or may not dive himself. The tender, or *kulaozeros,* is next in rank. He handles the divers on the bottom and is responsible for all the details of the diving equipment. Like the captain, he may or may not be a diver. Then there are one or two seamen, an engineer, and one or two ship's boys. Normally the divers—and there may be as many as twelve—do nothing but dive.

This pattern may be modified. The captain may double as engineer, and often all the men are divers. When the sponge fleet went to Africa, nearly everything had to be brought from Greece, since the boats sometimes worked for months off hostile shores without provisions or good harbors. In this case, a depot ship, usually a large schooner, accompanied the diving boats. In the North African fleet it was normal for one schooner to act as a mother ship to five diving boats. Meals were cooked and sponges cleaned on board the mother ship, and divers often slept there. Extra provisions could be carried by the mother ship, thus reducing the considerable clutter in the diving boats.

Sponge diving begins at dawn. As soon as it is light, the first diver goes over the side, after being outfitted on a bench, rigged on the starboard side of the bow. Once on the bottom, he gives the lifeline one jerk to announce to the tender that he is all right. He makes sure his hose is clear, and he looks around him. If the bottom is rocky, he will look for boulders, channels, or ledges where sponges might be.

The first sponge he spots gleams, black with reddish tints. It may be as far away as twenty feet, but it's easy to see in the clear water. It comes off easily, exuding a whiff of milky fluid. There will probably be others nearby, and as the diver pulls at the first, his eyes flicker in search of the second. Sponges grow in colonies, in places where the current is right. The factors that make it possible for sponges to exist in one place and not another are clear neither to divers nor marine biologists, but a good diver understands them by instinct. The best sponges grow on an eel-grass bottom, invisible under the grass, which may come to the diver's waist as he drags his hose and lifeline over the bottom. The trained eye sees the slight irregularity in the grass that indicates a sponge below.

The tender holds the lifeline above, watching the depth gauge attached to the cabin beside the clock, and follows the diver, feeling his movements as he walks perhaps a hundred feet below. After more or less than an hour, depending on the depth and the captain's judgment, the tender jerks the lifeline three times. The sailor who has been tending the hose on the starboard side pulls it in. The ship's boy drops the ladder and, as the diver comes to the side, helps him far enough up so that his helmet comes over the bulwark. The boy hugs it, twists, and the helmet comes off with a sign of air. Then he pulls the sponge bag over the side. If the dive has been a good one, the diver will need help.

Once the diver is on deck, there is a rush to remove the suit so the next man can use it. Very efficient boats carry a second suit, so that the second diver can be dressed before the first surfaces. In that case, only the breastplate and helmet need be transferred from the first suit.

Work goes on like this all day in a regular pattern. Everyone seems half asleep, but a vibrant alertness is just beneath the surface. A diver on deck can doze. The man tending the hose can never relax, nor can the captain and the men at the tiller and tender. If the lifeline was not well tended and the diver fell off a cliff underwater, he could plunge faster than the air could fill his suit, and he could be crushed by pressure. A diver's life very much depends on his tenders.

Over it all hangs the shadow of the bends. Unlike the hazards that affect other men involved in dangerous work, the bends are essentially undramatic. There is no romance in a bubble in your blood. Every diver in the trade has somewhere at the back of his mind a vivid image of the crippled shoeshine man in the Navarinon, the tapping canes of the Kalymnos waterfront, the screams or prayers or curses of a dying friend, the one the entire crew tried futilely to help, then buried, all the while thinking, "That could be me," and silently prepared for the next day's dives. The statistics of sponge diving even today are not cheerful. What they amount to is that divers cannot theoretically last twenty seasons without a good chance of being killed or crippled.

The strain of diving under this shadow makes for a wild month or two in the tavernas of Kalymnos when the fleet comes back in the late fall. It is a time for celebration, for marriage, new clothes, and good food. After the new year and the yearly sponge sale, owners and captains begin to bicker with their backers or the bank for the huge sums needed to finance a new voyage. The best divers will not sign on until their estimated shares are paid in advance. Then the crews begin to overhaul the boats, which have lain idle in the harbor all winter.

By Easter the boats are overhauled. The whole town turns out in a solemn ceremony of farewell, and the fleet sails. The married women put on mourning black.

Every year there are fewer mourning women, for the fleet continues to diminish. But the trade will probably never die completely, as long as the sponges are not struck with a greater blight than ever before, or some political cataclysm prevents seagoing in the Aegean for a generation or more, or the bottom doesn't drop completely out of the sponge market. There is more money in going to sea in steel ships, and a better future in emigrating to Australia, but island divers will continue to dive for sponges, although the trade will change. Today the old tradition of the helmet suit is giving way to free diving with the aqua-

Kalymnos harbor and part of the Kalymnian sponge fleet in the spring of 1961, ready to sail for the sponge banks of Bengazi. The first three boats from the left are aktarmades, *specially designed for diving platforms.*

lung; young divers are turning to the naval diving manuals for their instructions instead of to the old captains with their folklore.

Last year I was talking to a sponge-boat friend. We were sitting on a cabin top, drinking coffee, with a heap of glossy, black, acrid-smelling sponges on the deck below. He had left a good job in Australia to come back to Greece. I asked him why. He grinned as he answered, "That money didn't smell so good."

A helmet sponge diver is dressed aboard the Mandalinci, a Turkish sponge boat built on the Greek island of Symē before World War II. He then goes overboard to explore the Aegean bottom. A helmsman carefully watches for any tug on the rope that might signal trouble below.
Overleaf: The surfaced diver is pulled in with the lifeline by Captain Kemal Arras. Divers such as these are credited with the discoveries of most of the major Mediterranean shipwrecks.

The Treasures

What is the most spectacular underwater discovery? It is hard to say. I have long been cured, I hope, of gold fever, although it's probably an incurable disease, one whose symptoms must be suppressed in the middle of the most serious of underwater archaeological projects.

Yet treasure-hunting operations are inevitably commercial enterprises, in which the discoverers are forced to destroy what I feel is the real treasure: a new window on the world of the ancient mariners and the ships they sailed. For me, the most fascinating treasure ship yet found is the one that started all of us dreaming—the Roman argosy that sank off the Greek island of Antikýthēra, two generations before the birth of Christ.

The island of Antikýthēra lies in the middle of the mouth of the Aegean between Kythēra and Crete. The two islands and the reefs between them are salted with the bones of seamen. Even on a calm, beautiful spring day there is an ominous quality to the cliffs of Antikýthēra, which rise like a sheer wall from where the steep sandy slope stretching to the abyss begins two hundred feet below the indigo sea.

On September 17, 1802, the brig *Mentor* was driven on the rocks (where the sloop of war *Nautilus* suffered a comparable fate), at the entrance to St. Nicholas Bay on Kythēra, less than twenty miles to

---

Gold coins of the seventh century A.D. *Byzantine Emperor Heraclius, retrieved from the wreck at Yassi Ada. Sixteen such coins were found together; it is speculated that they were originally stored in the captain's cash box. The real Yassi Ada treasure: archaeologists George Bass and Frederick Van Doornink were able to re-create a Byzantine trading voyage. Opposite: Reverse of a coin of Antoninus Pius* (A.D. *86–161*) *depicting the Pharos at Alexandria.*

the north. She foundered in sixty feet of water with seventeen cases of marble on board. There was no loss of life, but the cases contained many of the friezes taken from the Parthenon by Lord Elgin. Within a month after the wreck sponge divers had been hired. It took two years before the cases were finally recovered.

Much has been written about the Elgin marbles, but it is hardly realized that one-third of them would not exist today if it had not been for the rough and ready men who dived naked sixty feet in order to salvage them. There is no record of how they worked and exactly what was done, except that Lord Elgin's representative on the island complained bitterly that he had endured much from the barbarous conduct of the divers—men who frequently took to drink. Musing over the letter to Lord Elgin, one wonders just what fiendish practical jokes were played by the wild men of the Aegean.

Ninety-eight years later, two little Symiot sponge boats, manned by descendants of the men who had salvaged the Elgin marbles, anchored in a bay at the north side of Antikýthēra to shelter themselves from a southwesterly gale that exploded into hissing clouds over the grave of the *Nautilus*.

Unlike their forebears, these men were equipped with the helmet diving gear that had been introduced to the Mediterranean just a generation before them. The larger of the two boats was what is called a deposito, a bigger schooner rigged up as a floating cookhouse, storeroom, and dormitory for the relays of men who worked from the little diving boat.

In the morning the weather broke a bit, although the sea was still rough. The captain, a young man from Symē named Dimitrios Kondos, took the diving boat around the cape, thinking that they might as well get in a few sponge dives instead of sitting idle until the sea calmed.

The water under the cliff was crystal-clear indigo blue, although the dying gale ruffled the water only a hundred yards offshore. Elias Stadiatis, the first diver, went over the side. The tender, crouched on the little bench in the bow with the hard-twist lifeline slipping through his fingers, could see the brownish shape of the diver for a long way as he sank toward the bottom. When the needle on the pressure gauge attached to the compressor stopped moving, it read thirty—thirty fathoms, or one hundred and eighty feet. Kondos turned the five-minute hourglass and instructed the men on the compressor handles to pump hard. At that depth a diver needed a lot of air.

In less than a minute the boy tending the hose shouted and the pressure gauge began to swing back. The diver was coming up, fast, before the five minutes that Kondos had allowed as a safe underwater period. The gleaming copper helmet broke water with a sign of escaping air, and the diver was pulled over to the ladder. He clambered up, and when the bulwarks were level with his waist, the ship's boy hugged the helmet, gave it half a turn, and pulled it off.

The men turned curiously toward the diver, wondering what had made him surface so quickly. A big

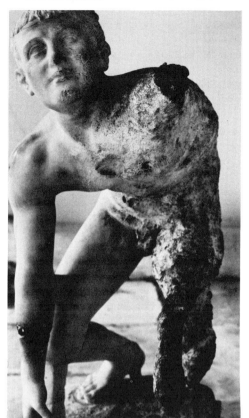

The island of Antikýthēra from Stormie Seas.

*Among the Antikýthēra finds were a life-size bronze head of a philosopher (page 82) and a first-century-*B.C. *copy of a classical discus thrower. The right side of the statue, which had been covered with sand for two thousand years, was in perfect condition. The exposed left was damaged by marine borers.*

shark? Or just a leak in the suit? Neither. It seemed that he was having some sort of fit, for he was gibbering, raving, frightened out of his wits.

They sat him on the dressing bench, and someone lit a cigarette and put it in his mouth. After the diver had taken a deep drag, Kondos again asked him what he had seen.

"Horse, naked women, upside down . . . dead, dead, all dead . . . rotten . . . something like a city. . . ."

That was all they could get out of him. Kondos dived himself and came up after the statutory five minutes, with a heavy greenish object clutched against his breastplate. Several pairs of hands reached for it and eased it over the low bulwark. It was a bronze arm, much corroded, and filled with sand and small stones.

The story might have ended there. Most captains would have left the wreck after grabbing whatever ob-

jects of value they could find, and the only evidence of the wreck might have been some handsome bronzes with sea marks on them, to be eventually displayed in a museum in Europe or the Americas. But Kondos was a man of more than ordinary schooling, who knew of the wonderful finds that were being made in archaeological excavations. In addition, he was a patriot, from Symē, which drew its entire living from the sea and which was still under Turkish domination like the rest of the Dodecanese. In fact, he was legally Turkish, and the ships under his command flew the flag of the moribund Turkish empire.

That November Kondos and Elias Stadiatis, wearing their very best suits and accompanied by a fellow countryman, Professor A. Economou, then a classics teacher at the National University, called on Spiridon Stais, the Minister of Education. With them, wrapped in a sack, was the arm. They told Stais that they were sure dozens of statues could still be found, as well as the rest of the bronze to which the arm had once been attached. They proposed that they be hired by the Greek Government to recover them. Stais, to his great credit, became an immediate partisan of their project, although many others in the ministry were suspicious; the whole thing seemed too incredible to be true.

His faith and the evidence of the bronze arm prevailed, and a few weeks later Kondos, Stadiatis, and Professor Economou were back on the site with a crew of divers and a Greek Navy transport. They were driven off the site by the weather after less than half a day of diving, and returned to Athens, carrying finds that sent the Athenian papers off into a rash of banner headlines: a life-size bronze male head, probably of a philosopher (now on view in the National Museum); the life-size arm of a boxer; and two marble statues that had been badly corroded by their long immersion.

Back again, they worked for a week. The *Michaelis* once again rolled back to Piraeus with a mixed bag of magnificent treasures, particularly a marble statue of a young boy, intact except for a missing right hand and foot. She also carried a colossal marble bull, a bronze lyre, bronze fittings for furniture, some bronze legs and marble hands.

During that winter the little group of sponge divers, supported by the Navy and continually plagued by horrible weather, explored the wreck. The story remained headline news; it was obvious to the whole world that this was a fabulous archaeological find. And, for once, this was a Greek expedition, not a foreign one. The only foreigners who had anything to do with the expedition were the Italian technicians who were called in to preserve the statues.

It was brutal work and a milestone in the history of diving. No one at the time, and few since, had understood what one hundred and eighty feet meant in terms of the knowledge of diving at the time. In 1902 the United States Navy regulations limited divers to sixty feet. The bends had been accurately explained fifteen years earlier, but the first calculated tables, giving the times divers could safely stay at various depths, were not published until four years after Antikýthēra.

In addition to the danger of bends, the divers contended with the narcosis of great depths, which turns the most stolid diver's fingers into thumbs. Air compressors of the type that Kondos' men used were to be condemned by the Royal Navy for use at depths beyond one hundred and twenty feet, because they did not give a large enough volume of air below that depth and compounded narcosis with lack of oxygen. It was to be four years before the Royal Navy did experimental dives to thirty fathoms with redesigned compressors.

The incredible fact about Antikýthēra is that these men, trained in the hard school of African sponge fishing, were able to take on a diving job that was beyond the capacity of any navy in the world.

By the first week of February the divers had established that they were working on the wreck of a big ship, parts of which still remained under the sand. The wreck lay parallel to the cliff on a sandy ledge only fifty feet from the sheer cliff. Just beyond the ledge a steep slope began, going down to a depth of more than one thousand feet, a half mile offshore. If she had not gone down like a stone when she hit the cliffs, the ship would undoubtedly have sunk in water so deep she would never have been found.

The bronzes were under a heap of stones which the divers at first thought were natural rocks fallen from the cliffs above, but which, on closer examination, proved to be badly corroded marble statues. Altogether there were parts of more than thirty marble statues, some weighing several tons. The finest object raised that winter, and the most spectacular of all the material eventually found, was a life-size fourth century B.C. bronze ephebus, now in the National Museum in Athens.

By the end of February most of the material that was visible had been cleared, and the divers were worn out. Work was temporarily stopped. It began again at the end of March, but the weather was worse than ever and little was accomplished. In the second week of April one of the divers got caught by the demon waiting at thirty-five fathoms. He came up from his second dive of the day gasping for breath, groaning and unable to speak. The captain sent ashore for a live chicken, which he killed and cut into two pieces and applied to the dying man's chest. It didn't work.

A life-size classical statue of Demeter found by Bodrum trawlers between Rhodes and the mainland of Turkey. It was this find that inspired the Bodrum Marine Archaeology project, begun by the author, which continues to this day under the direction of George Bass and the American Institute of Nautical Archaeology.

The Government requested the help of Italian divers from Genoa, who were said to be able to dive deeper and remain under water longer than the Greek sponge divers. The captains of the sponge boats protested and were given money to hire more divers. The new crews worked all summer long, until all the visible material on the surface had been recovered and it was no longer thought economical to continue. The work officially ended on September 3, 1901.

Dozens of theories about the wreck were proposed. One eminent scholar maintained that the ship was sailing from Argos sometime in the fourth century A.D., perhaps on its way to Constantinople. His effective argument silenced other points of view. One of the most easily explodable of the theories was the obvious one stemming from a passage in Lucian (Zeuxis 3) that describes a ship lost at Malea with a cargo of art works taken by Sulla, the Roman general, from the Athenian agora for shipment to Rome. The coincidence of a literary reference to the shipwreck found by the merest accident was too extravagant to merit such consideration, but later research established that it is indeed possible and perhaps close to probable. The domestic pottery, glass, and other small objects from the wreck can now be dated to the first half of the first century B.C. Among the small objects found in the wreck was a lump of sea-grown wood which split open as it dried out in the National Museum to reveal what seemed like clockwork. This find was studied by Derek de Solla Price, who concluded that it is a device for calculating the movement of the stars and planets and that it was made in Rhodes almost certainly in 82 B.C., the year that Sulla stormed the Colline gates and entered Rome after his successful conquest of Greece. It was last set in 80 B.C., so Sulla might very well have ordered this shipment of antique bronzes and "modern" marble copies of classical and Hellenistic originals.

The final chapter in the history of Antikýthēra has not yet been written. The site was visited in 1953 by Captain Cousteau in the famous research vessel *Calypso*. Chief diver Frederic Dumas made several exploratory dives on the site and found that a great deal of the actual structure of the ship was still there, under a few inches of sand. He concluded that the wreck was too deep for a modern archaeological excavation, as the depth will allow each diver only fourteen minutes of working time per day. Now modern developments in the techniques of diving make systematic work on the wreck possible, and in the next few years perhaps this work will be done. Then we will have the missing parts of half a dozen Hellenistic and classical bronzes and, most interesting, the small objects that will tell us who loaded that fascinating cargo, where and for whom, and in what ship.

The discovery of the Antikýthēra wreck was followed by others, equally spectacular. In 1908 Greek sponge divers found another Roman argosy, stuffed with goods for the Imperial art market, at Mahdia in the Bay of Tunis. In 1927 a trawler hung his nets on the arm of the greatest archaic bronze statue of all, at Cape Artemisium at the northern end of the Greek island of Euboea. Then, in the Strait of Messina that separates Sicily from Italy, Italian sports divers found and looted another classical wreck full of bronzes; one, perhaps by Praxiteles, is rumored to be for sale in Germany for a cool million dollars. David Owen, of the University of Pennsylvania Museum, surveyed the site in 1968 and found nothing but tantalizing fragments.

A king's ransom in gold and silver was salvaged in the 1960s after a retired house carpenter, Kip Wagner, discovered the remains of the Spanish fleet that had been driven ashore in Florida by a hurricane in 1715.

Opposite: *The sea destroys and the sea preserves: In 1970, we excavated the Porto Longo, Methone, site of HMS* Columbine *that had been lost in 1824. Found safely preserved in the soft mud were, among other things, blocks and a locker door.*

Left: *The Greek island schooner* St. George, *built in the early 1900s, is now bereft of her masts and rigging, though her fine decoration at bow* (top) *and stern* (bottom) *still survive as reminders of her past glory.*

But because the worth of the classical bronzes found in the sea is so enormous, marine archaeology has suffered. The Greek archaeologists who supervised the Antikýthēra operation were interested in the art objects; commercial treasure hunters are interested solely in the gold. Only a few expeditions have produced the true treasure: the ship, and the story of her last voyage.

The True Treasure

On the strength of the success of the Cape Gelidonya excavation, George Bass obtained funds for a more ambitious project: the excavation of the wreck of a cargo carrier of c. 620 A.D., which lay in one hundred and twenty to one hundred and forty feet of water at Yassi Ada. The ship had been loaded with round amphorae, which probably contained wine or oil. She lay in a bed of mud, and a good deal of the wood of the hull remained. The site was about thirty feet by seventy feet, much larger than the Cape Gelidonya site.

Bass and his crew built a camp on the deserted island where the ship had gone down, moored a hundred-ton barge over the wreck, and went to work. Most of the first year was spent in doing an exact plan of the surface layer of the wreck. This resulted in a redesign of the steel frame system developed for Gelidonya but not used there. The new frame was made of steel pipe sections assembled into measured squares. These stood on legs driven deep into the bottom and were stepped down the slope so that they were at no point more than one meter from the bottom. Each square was exactly horizontal. Photographs were taken with an underwater camera, fastened in a movable frame which put it at a fixed distance above the wreck for every picture.

The photographs were developed and printed immediately, and the distortion inherent in the camera's lens was calculated and corrected. The plan could then be made directly from the photographs, saving the laborious process of making measured drawings by hand on the bottom. By the end of the 1962 season this frame system was working well enough so that the plan, on a one-to-ten scale, was accurate to the thickness of the pen lines in the final drawing.

With the frame system Bass and his crew were able to dig right down into the wreck, recording as they went. They found the cook's pots, the ship's water jar, and the pay chest containing bronze coins and four gold coins which definitely dated the wreck to the first quarter of the seventh century A.D. Near it were two bronze steelyards for weighing cargo, one with the captain's name engraved on it: "George the Elder, Senior Sea Captain." Again, the importance of the objects is not in the objects themselves but in their context, allowing plans to be made which in turn will permit partial reconstruction of the ship on paper.

The excavation was a milestone in the history of undersea work as well as in marine archaeology. It was the first time in history that a technically complicated scientific operation on that scale had been carried out in deep water, and it proved conclusively that an underwater excavation could be carried out to land standards.

Survey teams sponsored by the University of Pennsylvania Museum discovered dozens of other shipwrecks in the Aegean, several of which were excavated. In places where the depth or shape of the bottom have prevented scattering of the ship in the immediate years after its sinking, these wrecks have been surprisingly well preserved. Those on muddy harbor bottoms, even in shallow water, have been silted over and are in remarkably good condition.

It seems that in temperate waters a wreck consolidates within fifty years. The exposed wood is destroyed by teredos and other marine organisms, and various chemical and biological processes continue to occur until the wreck is covered by a layer of mud, sand, or calcium carbonate growth. Then the process of destruction slows or, with some materials, stops altogether. Unless marked by large, imperishable objects such as cannon or clay jars, wrecks of wood ships are invisible after this consolidation, although it may be possible to locate them by observing changes in the contours of the sea bottom.

The Methone wrecks were interesting examples of the consolidation process. Both were wooden sailing ships of about three hundred tons burden; one sank in 1940 and the other in 1860. The 1940 wreck is not so well preserved as the 1860 one, although it lies in slightly more shallow water and parts of it are still visible above the muddy bottom. The 1860 wreck was completely invisible under a layer of mud from three to twelve feet deep. She had sunk with a heavy port list. The starboard side had almost disappeared, but the port side was intact for nearly fifty feet under a protecting coat of mud. The oiled finish on the bulwarks was still visible. The bulwarks themselves, the cap rail, a gunport, the blocks for pulling the cannon to the port, a belaying pin, the taffrail, and part of the cap rail of the bulwark were still intact.

The survey of both these wrecks was set up as an ordinary base-line survey, carried out exactly as such a survey would be done on land except that the tools used were improvised for underwater work.

The triangulation method was used for the surveys of two ancient shipwrecks found on a rocky bottom at Methone, one a third century A.D. ship from Egypt, carrying a cargo of unfinished granite sarcophagi, the other that of what now appears to have been a medieval ship on its way to Italy from the Middle East with a cargo of columns from an abandoned Roman town. Triangulation worked on both these wrecks because they were in shallow water, where time spent underwater was not limited by the dangers of caisson disease, as at Cape Gelidonya and Yassi Ada.

Although underwater archaeology seems technologically complicated to the outsider, sometimes even to the informed outsider, such as a land archaeologist, there is little new in the tools used up to now. The airlift or mammoth pump first used in the nineteenth century is the principal digging tool. Our only contribution to airlift engineering is that we have built airlift systems easier to control than their predecessors. The problem of the technology of underwater archaeology is that of adapting already existing methods to increased efficiency in the medium of the sea.

The technical problems that have historically prevented us from working in very deep water have largely been solved in the past ten years. In 1964 the University Museum got the *Ashera*, a two-man submarine built by the Electric Boat Company of Groton, Connecticut, and specially adapted for underwater photogrammetry. Today there is a whole stable of minisubmarines available to the undersea explorer, but their use is limited by their cost. The same is true for *Sea Probe*, a fantastically sophisticated ship that can drop a pipe equipped with a television, still cameras, and excavating tools to great depths. The trouble is that *Sea Probe* costs more for one day's use than the Cape Gelidonya excavation cost all summer.

There is evidence that deep wrecks are much better preserved than the ones we have worked on to date. The rate of deterioration of wood and metal diminishes with the decreased oxygen content of deep water and with the temperature drop, and deep-water sedimentary ooze would make an ideal bed for preserving a shipwreck. Such wrecks, under this ooze, will be hard to find, but prototypes already exist of the detection equipment that will make possible the finding of wrecks completely covered with mud. Once found, they need to be excavated, and the key to excavating underwater is underwater surveying, the simpler the better.

Diver Nikos Kartelias explores the remains of an Austrian brig that went down in the Porto Longo harbor of the island of Sapienza in 1860. Her stern, which had been covered with five feet of mud, was still intact and the oil finish on the bulwarks shining. Nikos fingers the belaying pin that held the spanker sheet and points to what was the level of the deck. A wooden davit for the small boat that hung over the stern is visible at the top left of the photograph.

Right: *A small ship with a cargo of four granite sarcophagi set out from Assos (near present-day Izmir) for Italy at the end of the third century* A.D. *She never made it farther than Methone, where she finally went down. We had hoped to find a bit of pottery or glass, that could date the wreck, under one of the lids, but we were unsuccessful. Here, John Bullitt, left, and Nikos Kartelias, right, use a set of double tanks to inflate lifting balloons attached to the lids of the coffins.*

Overleaf: *The airlift acts as a giant vacuum cleaner. A light sheet metal or plastic pipe is hung in the water from a buoy on the surface. Compressed air is pumped into the bottom end. As the pressure on the surface is less than that on the bottom, the air rises through the pipe, creating a suction at the bottom end.* Left: *Terry Vose cleans sand and seaweed off a cargo of Roman marble at Torre Sgaratta.* Top right: *A heavy airlift moves mud from the Austrian brig at Porto Longo.* Bottom right: *An airlift is rigged at Porto Longo. This particular airlift was made from galvanized sheet steel irrigation pipe, clamped together in fifteen-foot sections.*

Pages 94–97: *The cargo of a ship that sank in forty feet of water at Torre Sgaratta during the second century* A.D. *consisted of roughly cut sculptural marble from Aphrodisias, Asia Minor. It is believed that the ship was on its way to Rome. When she was found, she and her cargo lay under a five-to-ten-foot layer of sand, which was removed by airlifting. In order to study the ship's hull, we then had to remove the marble blocks—which weighed up to five tons each. A cluster of lifting balloons, filled with compressed air through a hose from a surface compressor, was lashed to each block with chains. As the air in the balloons expanded, their speed increased and tons of marble roared to the surface.*

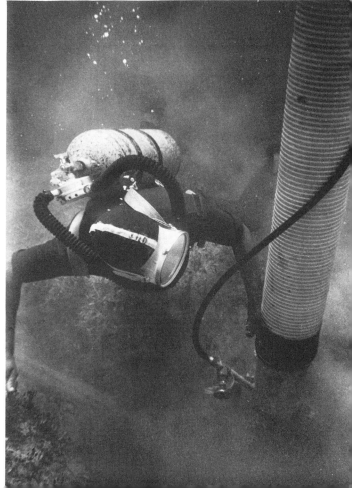

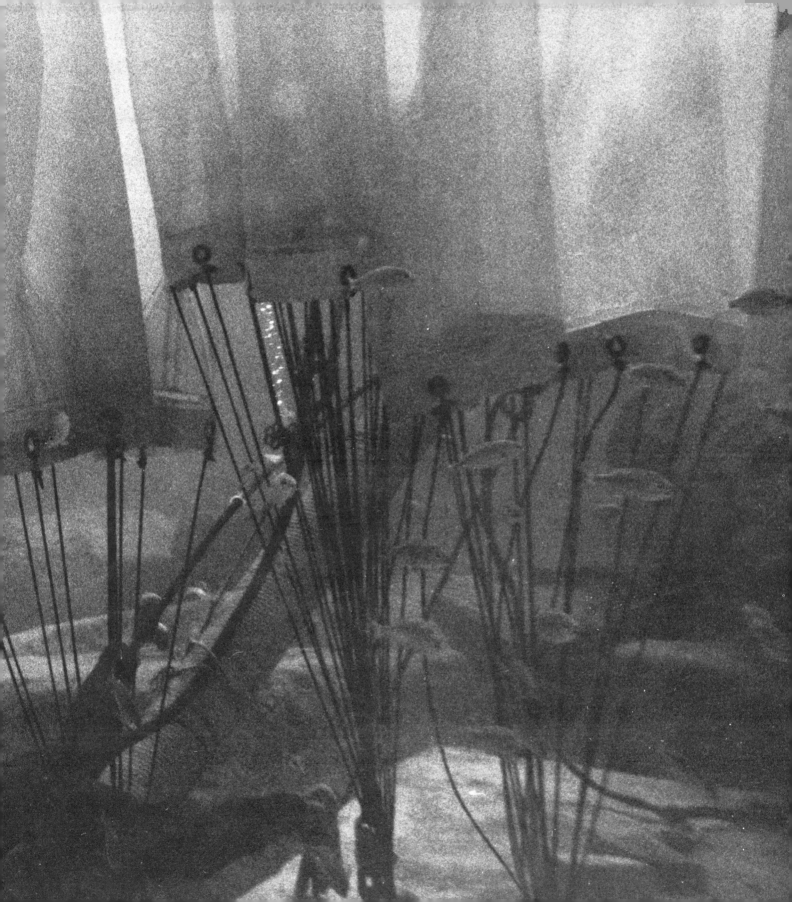

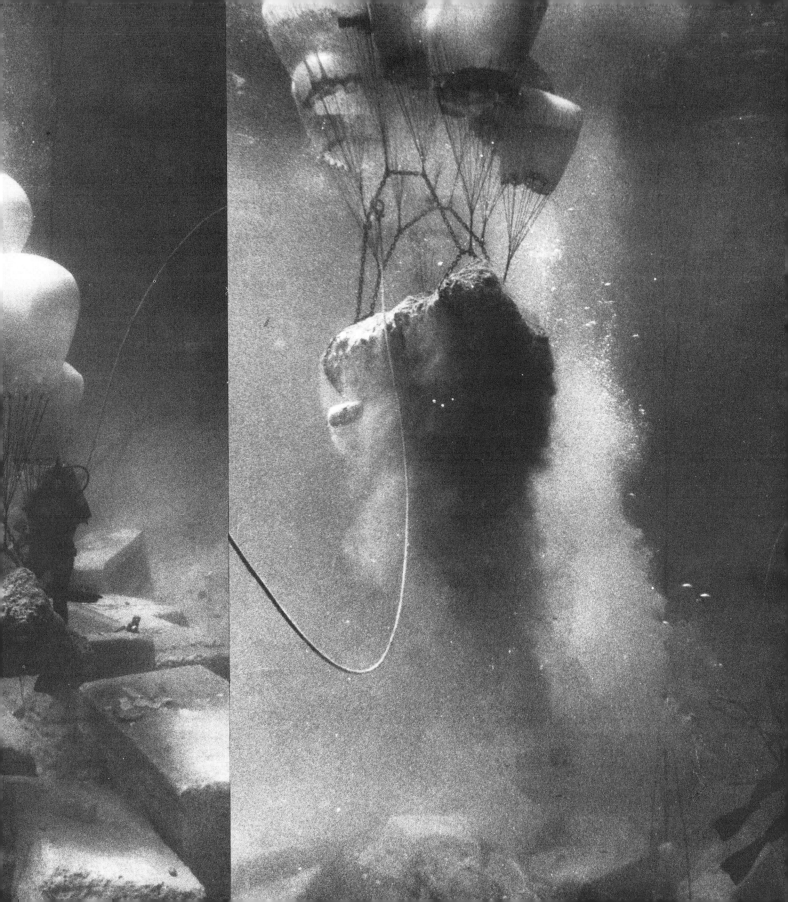

Above, top: Archangel *hovers over the wreck site. Note the surfaced lifting balloon, and the bubbles issuing from the bottom where we were at work.* Above, bottom: *Cargoes of marble were common in ancient times. Over a dozen have been found in the Mediterranean alone. This column capital, which originated in Asia Minor, was part of the finds of the fifth-century-A.D. Marzamemi wreck in south Sicily that Gerhard Kapitän excavated. The column was part of a prefabricated early Christian church.*

Once the marble blocks were raised from the site, they were moved to the "junkyard," where they awaited the arrival of the Italian Navy crane that would lift them onto dry land. All the blocks were raised in one day, allowing us to continue working on the site at our own pace without having to risk damaging the delicate wood that lay under the marble.

Simple Underwater Surveying and Photography

Beginning in 1962, Roger Wallihan and I investigated a series of shipwrecks, three of which were Roman ships that carried cargoes of rough-cut sarcophagi on their way to Rome from Greece and Asia Minor. Unlike cargoes of amphorae, these cargoes of stone contained a limited number of regularly shaped large objects.

We obtained reasonably accurate results by using simple land surveying methods underwater, with no instruments other than simple surveyor's tools obtainable in any reasonably stocked village store: carpenter's levels, plastic hoses, tape measures, and the like.

The first wreck we surveyed was the column wreck found off Sapienza Island in the southwestern Peloponnesus in 1962. As circumstances prevented our return to the site, we were unable to complete our studies. However, the methods described below were developed then and, with minor improvements, are still used today.

Surveying the Column Wreck

The seventeen columns lie scattered over an area approximately twenty meters wide by thirty meters long, on the rocky bottom that slopes from the northeast cape of Sapienza Island. The contours of the bottom skewed the columns in different directions when the ship that carried them disintegrated, or when they rolled off the ship's deck as it pounded on the point.

The upper end of the first column lies in the most shallow point of water, seven meters down and thirteen meters from the nearest point on the shoreline. The deepest, the seaward end of the seventeenth column, lies in twelve meters. The relative shallowness of the site proved to be both an advantage and a hindrance to the surveying team. The length of time a diver could spend underwater was not limited by the dangers of caisson disease, the so-called bends, and no time had to be wasted in lengthy decompression after a dive or in an enforced long interval between repetitive dives. Indeed, the only practical limitations on the amount of time spent underwater were the availability of compressed air and the cold. Even in the warm waters of the Ionian Sea in August, and with the protection of neoprene rubber jackets, few divers could work efficiently for more than an hour and a half at a time. But after a short period on the surface in the sun the divers could return to their work. If the shallow water was a blessing from the point of view of allowable time on the site, it had the distinct disadvantage of subjecting the men to the forces of surge. In order to use instruments on any single point, the diver had to be very heavily weighted, which, of course, limited his freedom of movement between points; instead of swimming underwater the weighted divers had to crawl on hands and knees from point to point, a risible sight but time-consuming and tiring.

From the beginning it was apparent that a photographic survey was an inadequate means of describing the site. The columns were too heavily overgrown with algae, sponges, and other sea growth difficult to remove, for a photograph, even with a scale in the picture, to give an accurate impression of an individual column. The area in which all the columns lie is too large to be covered by one photograph, and although the waters of Methone Bay are clear, the limits of visibility made it impossible to see from one end of the wreck to the other. Accordingly, a plan, carefully drawn to scale, seemed the best means of making a permanent record of this interesting ancient shipwreck.

In setting up our survey we attempted to apply the same standards of accuracy and to use the same methods of instrumentation that have proved successful on land. The most desirable method, from the standpoint of both accuracy and time, would have been a transit and tape survey. The transit can take horizontal and vertical angles by use of the instrument alone. A "one-minute" transit (i.e., a transit calibrated to 1′ of arc), used correctly, makes it possible to obtain an accuracy of one in 3000—that is, a maximum error of one centimeter at any given point in a site such as the column wreck. However, no underwater transit was available to us, and we had neither time, facilities, nor funds for the construction of one.

A second possible method—that of using a plane table—could have given us an accuracy of one in 1000, or a maximum error of three centimeters at any given point. One of the disadvantages of plane table surveying is that considerable time is required in the field. The "field" in our case was under water and time was at a premium. For this reason the use of the plane table was abandoned by Bass in his work at Yassi Ada in 1961.

A third possible method, and the one finally chosen, was a simple tape survey. This could have been nearly as accurate as a transit survey, but was subject to inaccuracies arising from the problems involved in handling tapes and levels underwater.

Tape surveys are based on a simple geometrical principle. Given the length of three sides of a triangle, the angles can be calculated. Or, if one measures to an unknown point from two known points, the location of the unknown point can be fixed. A measurement from a third known point gives a good check on any such triangulation, for the third point creates two additional triangles, each of which has as its apex the unknown point. The first step in our survey was, therefore, to set up a series of known control points. We selected the six highest rocks in the area, and at least two of them were visible from each unknown point. Once the control points were picked, measurements were made between them, and they were marked to scale onto the drawing board. The columns were then numbered with fiberboard plaques attached to them with steel wire.

Now that we had plotted our six control points, the next step was to measure the horizontal distance between them and the ends of the columns, or "unknown" points. Several problems arose. On land, this measurement would have been simple, because it would have been possible to measure horizontally from the fixed point to a plumb line held over the unknown point. We attempted to do this underwater by using a plumb line in reverse, a buoy anchored by a lead weight to the point we wished to locate. This did not work because the buoy was affected by both surge and current. The solution to the problem lay in another simple geometric principle: given two sides of any right-angled triangle, the length of the third side can be solved by the Pythagorean theorem $(a^2 + b^2 = c^2$, or the sum of the squares of the two legs of any right-angled triangle is equal to the square of the hypotenuse of the triangle).

All vertical measurements were taken in relation to control point three, the highest and most centrally located point in the area. We constructed a level plaform on point three, using an ordinary carpenter's level and a sheet of plastic supported by stones and held down with lead diving weights. Two nails driven to an equal length into the top of the level served as a sighting device. From point three it was then possible to sight with the level to a ranging rod held at each of the other control points and at each of the column ends or "unknown" points; the ranging rod had been calibrated in centimeters, and the vertical distance from the point to the horizontal plane of point three was measured on it. With the resulting data it was, of course, easy to compute the vertical height between any control point and any nearby unknown point. In most cases, we could establish the hypotenuse of our triangle by measuring directly the distance between the control point and the unknown point we wished to plot. Once the lengths of these two sides were determined, it was possible to use the

Pythagorean theorem to calculate the third side—the distance of a horizontal plane between the control point and the vertical projection of the unknown point.

Sometimes, however, it was impossible to measure directly between the control point and the unknown point because of an obstruction, such as a boulder or another column between the two points. When this happened, we used our carpenter's level to hold the rod as vertical as possible over the unknown point and measured directly to the rod with the tape. This system was not nearly so satisfactory or so accurate as the Pythagorean method described above, because the diver who held the rod had a hard time keeping a stable position in the water. When he stopped swimming in order to concentrate on the level, he either sank, rose, or was moved by the surge, and his level went off. When he concentrated on swimming, the vertical rod leaned. The spectacle of the diver, hanging in space on top of an aluminum pole with loops of tape floating around him while he thrashed feebly in circles trying to make the little bubble stay in the right place, was amusing, but the situation did not contribute to the accuracy of the survey. Several attempts had to be made for every measurement taken in this way, and the results of these measurements leave something to be desired.

Once the horizontal and vertical measurements to the end of the columns had been made, it remained only to measure the columns themselves. This was done just as it would have been done on land, with the additional complication that it was often necessary to clear off sea growth before it was possible to measure. The measured lengths of the columns gave an additional check on the triangulation measurements we have described, the length of the column as when triangulated using one side of an additional triangle. In addition to the length, the diameter was measured horizontally and vertically, whenever possible, at each end. The circumference was also measured at each end and used to calculate an additional measure of the diameter. Two or three measurements of the diameter were desirable because of irregularities in the manufacture of the columns. Measurements were also taken of the astragals of the columns. These, too, were irregular and required several measurements. In many cases the lie of the columns prevented some of these measurements from being taken.

When we had measured the columns and completed the triangulations, the information was plotted onto the scale drawing. It was then easy to see when a given point was suspect. If the two control points and the unknown point fell in a straight line, or nearly so, the check given by the control points being at a good angle[1] was lost, and instead of having three triangles to locate the unknown point, we had only two. Poor measurements resulted in a single point plotting at three points on the plan. If these three points were farther apart than the allowable accuracy of the survey, new measurements of triangulations were made.

The horizontal projection of each column was drawn from the measurements of length, diameter, and the relative elevations. These projections were placed on the plotted points and a plan view of the site was drawn. With the aid of an overlay photograph the rocks were added.

The accuracy of the drawing, exclusive of the rocks and contours of the bottom, is approximately ±10 centimeters. Several columns may not be better than ±20 centimeters,[2] but most are better than ±5 centimeters. We did not feel that it was useful for the

---

[1] *A strong triangle has no angles smaller than 30 degrees.*
[2] *Errors of this magnitude are rare and could have been corrected if sufficient time had been available.*

purposes of this survey to plot the contours of the bottom exactly. The bottom contours and rocks shown in the plan are much less accurate than the columns, due to their having been drawn from photographs. The two factors that contributed most to the inaccuracies of the final drawing were the difficulty of holding the rod vertical and the crudeness of our instrument (a carpenter's level) for taking levels. Experiments in measuring to rods held vertical with the aid of the level showed that the rod would vary from the vertical ±5 centimeters in 2 meters. Experiments with our instrument for shooting levels showed that our readings would vary ±10 centimeters in 10 meters. The combination of these factors, together with human error, prevented the survey from being as accurate as we could have wished.

Possibilities for Improvement

The most accurate existing method for surveying an underwater site is certainly the Bass-Duthuit-Dumas modification of the drafting frame first used underwater by Ferrandi and Lamboglia at Spargi in 1957. With a site as large as that of the column wreck, however, the expense of setting up such a frame is probably not justified by the increase in accuracy. The answer to the problem of surveying underwater sites as large as the Sapienza column wreck is probably a modification of the methods we have here described, with the possible additional use of the frame when small areas within the wreck are excavated. An improved instrument for taking the levels could be built cheaply. This instrument, combined with improved procedures in making the measurements, could improve the accuracy of a survey such as that of the Methone site to ±3 centimeters. Many small things can be done to improve the accuracy of such a tape survey. Pipes should be set in to use for control points. These pipes should extend above the surrounding rocks so as to give greater ease in measuring. An average increase in accuracy of ±3 centimeters could be expected. The points measured too could and should be better defined, perhaps by using underwater paint. This too should increase the accuracy by approximately ±3 centimeters. The measuring tape used at Methone was a commercial plastic tape, of unknown elastic properties. Calibration of this tape at a given tension against a surveyor's chain would have increased our accuracy by approximately ±1 centimeter.

In some instances it will still be necessary to measure to a vertical rod. In these cases extra measurements and greater care by the divers will be necessary to attain the desired accuracy.

With the experience gained at Methone, it will be possible in the future to make many more measurements in the same working time. The total *effective* working time, figured in man hours, spent underwater on the column site, was about thirty-seven hours.[1] About twenty additional hours were wasted in experimenting with methods that failed to work and in repeating early measurements that were inaccurate due to the divers' unfamiliarity with the method. These twenty hours would have been put to better use in the preliminary setting up of the survey. If more time had been available to us, it would have been possible to make many additional measurements, such as distances between columns. These would have given many extra checks and greatly improved our accuracy.

The total engineering and drafting time, not

---

[1] *The time (in man-hours) was spent approximately as follows: setting up control points, one; labeling columns, six; measuring objects, eight; shooting levels, four; tape triangulation, sixteen; photography, two; total effective diving time, thirty-seven.*

103

counting the time spent under water, was approximately one hundred hours. With the team's present experience this amount could be much reduced.

Due to working conditions on shore at Methone, it was impossible to plot all the measurements immediately, and some were even plotted after we left the site. The delay was unavoidable, but it impaired our accuracy. Overlays and detail photographs should have been developed and printed on the work site; they should have been available for study within twenty-four hours after they were taken, as at Yassi Ada and Cape Gelidonya. If we were to begin a similar project, we would sacrifice diving time to set up a drawing office and photographic laboratory in advance.

Leveling

The same year that we were experimenting with taking levels with carpenter's level and range rod, Don Rosencrantz, an engineer on George Bass's staff at Yassi Ada, made a simple adaptation of a land technique often used by masons to get levels. This was a hose full of water, which must remain at the same level in a length of hose so long as both ends are open. Rosencrantz pointed out that a bubble of air on the sea bottom would work the same way.

This method requires two divers and a long piece of transparent plastic hose. The first diver takes his end of the hose to the zero reference point. The second diver carries his end to the object whose level is to be measured. Both divers remove their mouthpieces and

blow air into the hose until it floats in an arc between them. The meeting place between air and water in the hose at each end should now be visible as a line near each end of the hose. The first diver now holds the line at his end at zero point, while the second diver measures the height between the object and the air-water interphase line at his end.

A recent improvement on this method is a gadget built by Robert E. Love for a survey of a series of Roman anchors found in the Aeolian Islands off Naples. His method involves a sensitive depth gauge, set to zero point, which reads depth relative to zero with a high degree of accuracy. Love's differential depth system is undoubtedly the most efficient way of getting relative levels on an underwater site. This

Producing good underwater drawings is a necessary part of marine archaeology. One of the tricks invented by surveyor Roger Wallihan at Methone was to build an improvised surveyor's level with rocks, and a sheet of plexiglass and a simple carpenter's level with two nails stuck in it as a sighting device. We found that it was possible to make accurate surveys of underwater sites with simple methods like this.

John Bullitt and Roger Wallihan set up the leveling device. The diver on the carpenter's level signals when his finger is on the datum point; thus a measurement of the height of the object in relation to the datum point is obtained. This method works very well in clear water.

combined with a hand sonar system, which would make automatic read-out measurements and eliminate the use of a metric tape, would simplify underwater triangulation enormously. The basic principle remains the same.

Triangulation works whenever you have a fairly concentrated site within a reasonable area. (That is, a base-line survey is going to be easier and better on a very long thin site, for example.) Measurements made with tapes over ten meters are going to be increasingly inaccurate as the distance grows, affected by current, obstructions, unknown elasticity of the tape used over a period of time underwater, and so forth.

One thing to remember when triangulating is to be sure that control points have been fixed outside the site.

The excellence of triangulation, from the amateur's point of view, is that involvement with mathematics is minimal. Every measurement can be plotted directly to scale on the drawing. It is, incidentally, better to use a metric tape or chain than one marked in inches, since metric measurements are much easier to reduce to scale on the drawing.

Base-line Surveys

A base-line survey works well on a site spread out on a flat bottom when it is much longer than it is wide. One begins by driving permanent stakes in at each end of the site and stretching a rope between them, making sure that the rope is outside the site. It is preferable to use nylon rope, which will stretch but keep its elasticity, so that the base line is always tight. Once the base line is laid, a metric tape can be laid along it. One then measures objects at right angles to the base line.

It is easier than one might think to get the measuring tape at right angles, especially when the distance to be measured is under five meters and the water is clear.

This method requires two divers, one to hold the tape on the base line and write down the distance on that line, the second to measure the distance of the object from that line. (Thus your object will be, for example, 3.60 meters from the base line at point 1.20 on the base-line tape.)

We have sometimes used combinations of base line and triangulations surveying, such as the survey we ran on a wreck in Porto Longo, at the other end of Sapienza Island from the column wreck. This was a wooden ship called the *Heraclea*, which we wanted to study in order to see how the wreck was breaking down.

We drove a steel peg into the bottom on each corner of the wreck and stretched a nylon line between the four corners. We then triangulated the main part of the wreck from the four stakes and worked out details, using the nylon ropes stretched between the stakes as base lines. This was possible at this particular site because the ship was on an almost flat bottom and it was not necessary to take levels.

Ship Sections

On a shipwreck site we have generally found that a series of sections give a very good idea of the shape of the ship. Plans of shipwrecks, especially when most

---

Photo mosaics are essential companions to accurate measurements of underwater sites. They consist of dozens, sometimes hundreds, of vertical photographs taken at a fixed distance over the site. In this photograph, Joan Throckmorton works out details for her drawings from the photo mosaic of the Pelagos site.

of the surviving structure of the ship has disappeared under the mud, do not give a very good idea of what the ship was like. Sections always do. Often a simple section done through the surviving part of the wreck makes it possible to reconstruct the ship at that section from bulwark to keel.

These sections are easy to make. Once a plan has been made of the wreck site, or, in the case of a wreck that is completely covered with mud, once the approximate lie of the keel is known, stakes can be driven in outside the wreck at approximately right angles to the keel. These stakes should be very secure —as deep as a strong man can drive them in. Once the stakes are in, on either side of the wreck, a line is stretched between them and each end of the line measured to mean low-water or high-water level.

A trench is then airlifted along the line of the rope, down to the timbers of the ship. Once the ship is exposed, a tape can be laid along the line and, as in the base-line survey, measurements made every ten centimeters or so from the base line down to the timbers. At the same time, each timber is measured, starting from one side of the excavation.

This method is especially useful for exploratory work with a small budget, when one wants to establish the kind of wreck being dealt with.

Obviously, in a wreck with a cargo that covers the hull, the cargo must first be removed. It would be nonsense to section a Mediterranean wreck full of amphoras until the wreck, with cargo, had been drawn in plan. However, sectioning is probably the only practical way of working on a wreck in a tideway —for example, in English waters, where it might be impossible ever to clear a wreck completely.

Sometimes one runs into sites so large that they require a combination of all the available simple methods. An Iron Age village at Lake Bolsena, north of Rome, was such a site. The visible remains consisted of dozens of house posts surrounded by hundreds of broken pots on a muddy bottom fifteen feet deep, a quarter of a mile offshore.

We decided on an underwater base-line survey combined with triangulation. In order to be able to relate our plan to a map of the region and the modern shoreline, we asked a professional surveyor and engineer to shoot the locations of the principal points, such as the ends of the base line and the house posts we were using as triangulation points. He then plotted these on a master plan. This was easily done from a theodolite position on shore, since the water was only fifteen feet deep and a pipe, held upright by a buoy and fastened to the various points in succession, could be used as a target.

Once our control points were in, we measured the position of posts that had not been fixed by the theodolite, in relation to the control points. We then divided the site into triangles, whose apexes were house posts. These triangles were seldom larger than a couple of meters on their longest side. We then sent teams consisting of a draftsman and an airlift operator to each triangle in turn. They then drew the finds in relation to the triangle boundaries, a modification of the base-line system.

On this site photogrammetry would probably have been impractical, since the water was often very dirty. But it did not matter. In fifteen feet of water there is time for careful drawing.

A point that cannot be emphasized too strongly is the necessity of marking every object that must be recorded on any underwater site. This is necessary if objects are to be lifted, if (as always) measurements must be checked, if a group of objects are to be drawn in relation to one another, and absolutely obligatory when (as nearly always) the drawing is done not by a single person but by a relay of draftsmen. This especially applies to ship timbers.

In examining any underwater site, it makes sense to begin by laying down control points and/or a base line before any other work is done. Sketch drawings, uncontrolled photographs, and miscellaneous measurements tend to be useless unless they can be keyed into a pattern.

All our Mediterranean surveys have been done with simple adaptations of land methods. Within certain limitations, these work well. The underwater excavator, often harassed by technical experts, is sometimes persuaded that working underwater requires elaborate special technique and instruments. It does not.

What it does require is ingenuity to adapt land principles to the underwater site. A professional surveyor can nearly always be consulted, who can set up a method for the given site, which can be carried out by divers with a minimal knowledge of surveying. We have been fortunate in the advice of such architects and surveyors as Clifford Irish, Roger Wallihan, John Youngman, and Joseph Shaw, each of whom got reliable results from groups of semi-amateur divers, who knew nothing about surveying.

Airlifting

The airlift is the simplest and most effective digging device under water. All that is required is a sufficient length of pipe to reach at least twenty feet above the site, inclining at such an angle that the airlift spoil will not drop back down on the excavation. This pipe should be supported at its upper end by a small buoy which reaches the surface and gives positive buoyancy to the pipe, which should be supported at intervals by buoys floating under the surface. These buoys need not be regular nautical buoys. Anything airtight will serve—plastic five-gallon water cans, even empty glass containers. Remember:

1. An airlift's need for air increases swiftly as the depth decreases.

2. Airlift pipes should be light, preferably galvanized sheet steel, and as big as possible. Eight inches is a good diameter for most jobs.
3. The discharge should not go above the surface, remaining preferably a few inches under it, so as to avoid buffeting by waves. Filters are difficult to use and are generally to be avoided. Skillful excavation can almost always take the place of a filter.
4. Engineers can make marvelous calculations concerning airlift operation, most of which are not of much use to the underwater excavator.

A workable rule of thumb for an eight-inch pipe working in fine sand or mud is:

Under twenty feet—a big road-building compressor capable of running at least three jackhammers.
Between twenty and thirty feet—a two jackhammer compressor.
Between thirty and forty feet—one jackhammer.
Over forty feet—almost anything. Deep water requires very little air to make a good suction force in the pipe.
In hard mud, weedy or rocky sand, double the above volumes of air.

5. The efficiency of the airlift increases as the pipe approaches the vertical. In deep water, with a slight current, the airlift pipe can be vertical as the current will carry away the spoil. A site in, say, fifteen feet of water requires a long pipe to dump spoil on one side of the site, and a great deal of air to counteract the inefficiency caused by friction in the sloping pipe.
6. Avoid gadgets. They tend not to work.

A short length of rubber hose at the end of an airlift helps the diver reach difficult places. A long length of flex is worse than useless, since it will trap air and often flip the whole apparatus, disturbing and dangerous for both the site and the diver.

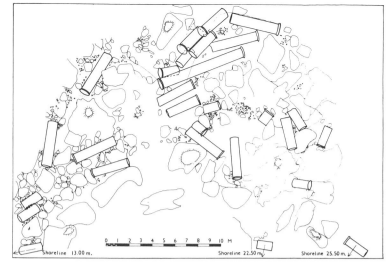

Handles are usually not necessary. The air supply hose can be simply tucked into the bottom of the lift pipe and pulled out when the diver wants to stop the lift. This also makes the air hose readily available for other purposes, such as filling the plastic leveling tube or filling lift bags.

An airlift of less than about four inches in diameter is not very useful, as it tends to get blocked by large shells or seaweed. The airlift must be supplied with sufficient air, so that the velocity of the air/water mixture in it is great enough to entrain the densest particles (if not, these particles tend to build up in the mouth, eventually blocking it). The necessary velocity is quite high, and as the smallest practical airlift is four inches in diameter, this means that airlifts are, as a species, pretty violent animals.

However, apart from moving more sand, a powerful airlift has the advantage—in clear water—of suck-

---

Top: *Roger Wallihan's survey of the column wreck at the north end of Sapienza Island. The columns were made of red granite that was probably quarried at Aswan, way up the Nile. The accurate drawing allowed us to establish that the columns had been broken when loaded onto the ship and that the ship was probably Venetian. It seems that they might have stood in the Roman port of Caesarea (in present-day Israel) from the time of Christ to the thirteenth century, when Crusaders destroyed a colonnade of similar columns in Caesarea and piled them up for a pier. Some, loaded several centuries later probably by a Venetian trader, were to be lost off Methone.*
Center: *Frames and planking found under marble blocks at Torre Sgaratta. Each timber is identified by a plastic tag with a code number.* Bottom: *Tagging a cargo of marble columns at Methone before the survey begins.*

ing away the clouds of sand and mud that are unavoidably produced by excavation. So, when delicate work is being done, a powerful airlift can be an advantage rather than a disadvantage, especially if the following method is used:

The mouth of the airlift is placed about eighteen inches away from the work face on a flat surface—such as a piece of wood or a stone slab—about two feet square, which prevents the airlift from burying itself. The work face is then carefully broken up by hand or with a knife and scooped toward the airlift when required. Breaking up the work face by hand, though it tends to be a bit painful if there are any sharp-edged shells in the sand, has the advantage that it is often much easier to detect changes in strata by feel rather than by vision. Any excavation always makes the upper layers of sand fall down, creating a curtain that obscures the work face.

Underwater Photography

Underwater photography is an essential part of any undersea excavation, and an impressive arsenal of undersea cameras and lenses is now available, from Edgerton, Gershausen and Greer deep-camera and strobe units that take good pictures five miles down, to the popular, simple, and indispensable Nikonos 35mm camera.

If money and talent are available, few underwater photographic problems cannot be solved.

The excavator of a wreck, like the excavator of any archaeological site, must record the locations of finds and make an accurate survey of the site. As diving times, even in shallow water, are limited, it is sensible to use photography as a recording tool wherever possible; however expensive photographic equipment may be, it is still cheaper than wasted diving time.

The making of drawings and plans on the bottom takes from a quarter to a half of the time spent underwater. It should obviously be done by photography rather than by hand, but there are technical difficulties, some of which are common to the general undersea photographer and film-maker as well.

The undersea excavator must never forget that it is the general public, in the final analysis, that pays for his excavation. When planning a project, the director should therefore keep various possible uses of photography in mind.

Simple Recording

All finds should be photographed in place as they turn up. Notes, no matter how good, never provide a complete substitute. But neither is a photograph a substitute for accurate field notes. This is especially true under water, where the excavator, his time often severely limited because of decompression problems, never sees the site in the same way as the land excavator does.

Working photographs must be processed on the spot, so as to be available to the excavator for study within a day of having been taken. This means having a portable darkroom, with someone to run it.

Photogrammetry and Mapping

Undersea mapping, by means of stereo pairs, was first suggested in the early 1950s and was first used effectively on an underwater excavation by Karius, Merrifield, and Rosencrantz under the direction of George Bass in 1964. A pair of aerial cameras mounted on a miniature submarine made it possible, within a few days, to collect the data needed to make an accurate map of a shipwreck.

When extreme accuracy is not essential, a grid system (for example, the grid developed by Professor Nino Lamboglia and used at Giannutri and Albenga) can be used. Although inaccurate, mosaic photographs, showing the whole site, are also useful.

Special Problems of Undersea Photography

Optics. A detailed discussion would fill several books. The basic problems are interrelated. They are:

1. Loss of lens efficiency or ability to resolve because of particles of plankton, mud, and so forth in the water.

2. Increase of the lens's focal length underwater because the water acts as an additional factor; e.g., a 28mm wide-angle lens mounted on a 35mm Leica Format camera becomes, under water, a 35mm lens. A 35mm lens on the same camera becomes a 50mm or normal lens, and so forth.

Obviously, the dirtier the water, the closer the photographer must come to his subject. The fact that the wide-angles lenses are less wide under water presents a problem, especially in very dirty water, where extreme-wide-angle lenses are required. This poses another problem if grid or stereophotogrammetry is to be attempted, because distortion increases as the angle of the lenses is widened. Up to the present, experiments in photogrammetry have been carried out in reasonably clear water, with the camera five to fifteen meters above the subject. Accurate stereophotogrammetry is probably not impossible in dirty water, using wide-angle lenses near to the subject, but it has not yet been successfully done.

3. Change in the character of light under water.

The sea acts as a blue filter. The spectrum is gradually filtered out until, at approximately ten meters, only blues and greens remain. Plankton in the water seriously reduce the amount of light reaching the bottom until black-and-white photography becomes impossible. With flash or strobe good pictures can be taken except when suspended particles in the water between the light and the subject create reflections.

The undersea photographer can use several devices to increase the quality of his photographs in dirty water:

1. Shooting black-and-white film at a high ASA rating and using a special developing process. For example, the amount of light on a site may seem to require an exposure of, say, f/3.5 at 1/30 second. If pictures are taken at this exposure and developed normally, exposure will be correct, but the pictures will probably be blurred because shot at 1/30 second, and the focus will be limited, as no lens has a satisfactory depth of field at f/3.5.

Instead, the photographer shoots at the most efficient lens aperture, say, f/8 or f/11, at a shutter speed of 1/100 second or more. He then develops the film accordingly. The slight loss in quality from pushing the film will be compensated by the added sharpness of the photograph; in addition, film developed at a high ASA rating often gives good contrasts. Additional contrast is nearly always desirable in underwater photographs because the light on the bottom is so diffused.

2. Flash systems which crosslight the subject from close up avoid the plankton particle reflection effect.

3. Using a plastic box full of clear fresh water in front of the lens (Bengt Borjesson, the only photographer to get good pictures of the *Vasa* under water, used this method).

In the case of wrecks in very cloudy water, it might well be possible to put plastic covering right over the wreck, and pump the areas to be photographed full of fresh water. Photographs could be taken right through the plastic. This experiment has never been tried!

Photographing a Large Site

Personnel: Photographer. He should be a professional photographer interested in diving rather than a diver interested in photography. He must run a darkroom on the spot and understand developing and printing. He should be skillful with underwater camera equipment, which needs much maintenance and proper care. The ability to teach and to work with other people is important, as he will have to delegate much of the actual photography to others.

Assistant. A student assistant from the archaeology section of the excavation, assigned part-time.

Filming: If working in color, the photographer will need a full-time, skilled assistant who is a competent mechanic and can operate the underwater lights, necessary on any site deeper than eight to ten meters.

The photographer and his assistant should do all the underwater filming, shooting events underwater as they occur. As local processing is impossible, the film should be shipped often, the processing laboratory reporting back to the photographer to allow a continual check on the quality of the exposed film. If this is not feasible before the end of the expedition, the photographer should process test strips himself—there is no point in shooting a whole roll of film only to discover, for example, that it is underexposed.

A shooting script should be worked out early. A certain period should be set aside each week for surface film work, as otherwise the continual presence of a cameraman will tend to disrupt the other work. The expedition director attempting a film for a television or other agency should ask for a first-class professional cameraman for the basic surface shooting. With the help of the producer, any good photographer can shoot good film under water but it takes real skill to shoot acceptable film on the surface.

Equipment. Any commercial 16mm camera with decent lenses will do. Even if shot for lecture purposes only, all film should be 16mm, at 24 frames per second; 8mm film, or 16mm at 16 frames, is commercially useless—the money saved will not compensate a lost opportunity of selling film for television purposes.

Color film for cinema work: high-speed Ektachrome Daylight for work in deep or dark water; Kodachrome is very satisfactory at other times.

Black-and-white: Eastman Tri-X or Gevapan Reversal 36, which can be developed to 500 ASA.

Journalistic and Scientific Photography

All journalistic material should be shot in both color and black-and-white. Below eight meters color should always be shot with a flash (PF5 daylight bulbs or equivalent), as should black-and-white where good contrast is required.

Film material: Color. Kodachrome II for 35mm seems more satisfactory than other color films, as it comes out in the blue spectrum better. Ektachrome commercial film is very satisfactory for the 120 format. *Black-and-white.* Kodak Tri-X and Plus-X should be used, as they can be manipulated in the darkroom better than most black-and-white films, and have good contrast.

A continual effort should be made to get good 35mm slides. They are invaluable for lecture purposes. Original slides are better and cheaper than duplicates. At the end of the expedition, the best pictures should be selected with a view to popular publication. The second-best are still available for lecture purposes—never the top selection, as they are invariably ruined or rendered unusable by bad projectors or unskilled operators.

Still Photography

We have found the 35mm watertight Nikonos or Calypsofot cases the most satisfactory, especially if proper care is taken in processing. The average expedition should have at least three Nikonos cameras, with flash equipment. A Rolleimarine or Hasselblad or other 120 camera should be available for close-ups of objects on the bottom, where better quality is required than that obtained with the 35mm format.

Reconstructing an Ancient Shipwreck

If the aim of my particular type of treasure diving is to reconstruct the ship, then the late Roman Empire ship found at Pantano Longarini is an excellent example of translating a mass of wood into a historical treasure, even though the work was done while wading in mud, rather than diving down to the wreck. I include this excavation because the Pantano wreck is the only ship that my group has yet managed to reconstruct from broken pieces found in the mud, although a study of the hull of the big Roman cargo carrier excavated at Torre Sgaratta is in the works.

Richard Steffey, ship specialist at George Bass's American Institute of Nautical Archaeology, has, along with Fred Van Doornink, managed to reconstruct the lines of the Yassi Ada on paper, as well as the Hellenistic ship found at Kyrenia, Greece. Ole Crumlin Peterson has successfully reconstructed the Roskilde Viking ships, using similar methods; in fact, an exact replica of one participated in "Operation Sail," New York's most elegant Bicentennial event. The replica, *Sebbe Als*, was lovingly built over a five-year period by a group of Danish schoolboys led by Karl Otto Larson. The reconstruction, accurate even to the tools and materials used by the Vikings of a thousand years ago, has sailed throughout Scandinavia and has contributed greatly to the understanding of what Viking ships of this type could do.

In diving for ships and drawing their remains, we are searching for the treasure of lost technology, techniques of secretive craftsmen of the remote past. It took a month to excavate the Pantano wreck, and a year of desk work before the material was understood well enough to write about it. The following account, excerpted from a 1973 issue of *The International Journal of Nautical Archaeology and Underwater Exploration*, was written by Joan Throckmorton and me.

The Pantano Longarini was probably once the anchorage known to Greeks as Odissea, to Romans as Edissa, and to Arabs and present-day Sicilians as Marza. There is a passage in Cicero *in Verrem* (ii, v. 34) that places the pirate ships in Edissa, and the Romans in the harbor of the ancient Pachinos, which is the present-day Pachino, a small town just to the west of Cape Passaro at the southeastern corner of Sicily. It is clear from various early texts that the whole low-lying area was once an extension of the sea. It is now silted up.

The wreck was discovered in the course of drainage operations that were part of a land reclamation project undertaken by Francesco Spatola, an imaginative farmer who had lost his land in Tunisia after World War II.

The workmen who first uncovered parts of the ship's structure took some of the cypress planking to a local shipyard and tried to sell it, so strong was the ancient timber. Through a series of coincidences not very remarkable in a small Sicilian village, the presence of the wreck came to the attention of the local archaeological authorities. An emergency grant was given by the University of Pennsylvania Museum, and our group undertook to excavate the site for Professor Bernabò Brea, director of the Syracuse Museum, with Gerhard Kapitän, who had brought the site to the attention of the authorities in the first place, and whose initiative made the whole project possible. When the wreck was discovered, Kapitän arranged for radio-carbon dating, which indicated 500 A.D., ± 150 years, as a date for the wreck.

We closed the end of the ditch so that the wreck lay in a shallow pool that could be kept dry with electric salvage pumps. Pumps of this type are essential for such an excavation, as they always keep their prime, and the rubber impellers are unaffected by sand and mud so long as the mud is dissolved in water.

The excavation revealed about thirty feet (9.1 meters) of the starboard side of the stern above the waterline of a large ship. The structure extended up to the side of the ditch, beyond which the excavators had dug up and destroyed more than half of it.

Several observations could be made immediately. The ship had an unusual kind of transom stern. The planking and wales which had been worked onto the stern were attached in an unfamiliar way. The ship was very heavily framed with grown timbers, roughly adzed to fit in place, so fitted that there was little space between the timbers. Heavy inner stringers had been fitted inside the frames. As in modern construction, frames and floors alternated, and light pine boards had been fitted between the stringers so as to close in the cargo hold and keep the bilges clean. The ship was iron-fastened throughout, with forged-iron nails and bolts, which had disappeared but left lumps of black mush surrounded by a concreted mold.

The unique feature of the construction was the manner in which one frame and two deck beams had been worked so that they tucked into slots cut for them in a heavy wales that ran along the sides of the ship. These frames and beams protruded outside the wales, which were massive half trees about half a meter thick. "Through beams" are an important detail of ancient ship construction, which had long been known from mosaics and sculptures, but which had never been studied in an actual shipwreck before.

It was evident from the start that the Pantano wreck was, like the Byzantine wreck recently excavated by the Pennsylvania group at Yassi Ada, an example of a transitional period in the history of naval architecture. This type of ship is still in the Roman tradition but has begun to take on medieval or modern characteristics. In fact, our extensive research in ancient shipbuilding was able to help us conclude the most interesting fact about the Pantano wreck: it illustrates a previously unknown type of transitional ship.

The first step in excavation was to tag every timber as it appeared. The tags, of laminated plastic, have a black layer in the center and white layers on the outside. The letters are cut through the white layer on one side. As the plastic is chemically inert and does not change color, the numbers are permanently visible, unlike painted numbers on tin and the like. We developed this system in 1965, for work at Lake Bolsena.

Each tag bears three letters, one of about six thousand three-letter groups from a combination of three alphabets. This idea was developed by George Bass at Yassi Ada in 1961 and 1962. The three-letter code is much easier to work with than a number code, both because there are fewer units, and because everyone instinctively looks for 2 to follow 1, and so on, thus suggesting a sequence of relationships which may not in fact exist.

Two steps then were carried out, more or less simultaneously. Three stakes were driven into the ground outside the wreck site, and from an arbitrary zero level on one of these, levels of the other reference points (the other two fixed stakes) and of each end of nearly every timber of the ship were then taken. This was done by means of a long plastic tube partially filled with water, the level being noted at the point where the water-air line corresponded with, or lay a measurable distance below or above, the chosen zero point on the first stake. Roughly three hundred and fifty levels were taken.

Once the levels were known, direct horizontal measurements could be made from each control point and the third side of the resulting triangle calculated so that we could transfer the measurements onto a plan.

A theodolite would have given a more accurate result, but, as we were without one, we used the crude water-hose method instead. Accuracy was sufficient for our purposes, especially as we were eventually to depend for fine lines on the matching of nail hole to nail hole on a model.

At the same time, two of the group drew each timber in relation to those surrounding it, locating and measuring each nail hole and tool mark as well. With a survey group of five (four after Kapitän was obliged to leave) we were working against time. The landowner was anxious to get on with his ditch. The weather steadily worsened, and even if it hadn't, we had reached the end of our funds. There was no question of returning the next season, since the ditch had to be cleared at once.

As timbers were photographed, measured, drawn, and their levels taken, they were removed in sequence. Once the cypress planking was exposed, we saw that we could count on it very well to tell where frames, floors, and other timbers had been placed. Nails that had fastened frames to the great longitudinal wales left round marks (incrustation surrounding nothing or a soft substance of decomposed iron) about two-tenths of a meter in diameter. Other timbers, lighter and less essential to the structural strength of the ship, had been fastened by square forged-iron nails, often driven in pairs. These smaller nails also held frames or floors to the hull planks which lay between the wales, odd and even, throughout the part of the ship that remained for us to study.

We drew up the wreck as well as we could on the spot. Three of us had drafting experience; in the aggregate, this was mainly underwater. Working on land or in a swampy ditch brought its own problems. Under water one always has a vertical line to which to refer, by tying a string to anything that will float, barring very shallow water, very strong current, or a very rough surface. Our muddy site would not stay clear nearly as long as an airlifted undersea site would. These are just two examples of the comparative peculiarities of working undersea and ashore.

As each timber was removed from the wreck for storage in fresh water, we drew sections of it, as well as we could manage. We did not get sections of every single timber, as we were short of good weather, time, and money. At the end, when the crane arrived to haul off the timbers by horse and cart, we measured as much as we could as fast as we could.

We feel that the ones we missed, the timbers without precise sections drawn, were those which were nearly the same as those adjacent to them, which were drawn. Still it would have been better to have returned to trace all the timbers onto plastic.

The original method we employed was to stretch a tape from one end of any given timber to the other, measuring the distance from the tape to top and bottom of the timber every few centimeters, noting constructional marks along the way. Timber by timber this was reasonably adequate; in the aggregate, it was probably quite satisfactory. Still, one would like a 1:1 tracing in order to *know* that no error had occurred because of windy weather, sagging tape, and other difficulties.

The wreck had opened out, both from the original catastrophe that sank her and from the weight of sand and mud that had rested on her for so many years. We could not reconstruct her lines on paper very well, as our principal source of precise information about her construction was nail holes: these differed one from another sufficiently in size and shape and patterned grouping, so that one could not say with confidence what job the fastenings had done.

Large through bolts fastened wales to frames. Smaller nails held frames to hull planking, or inner stringers to frames. At various decisive points along the hull, some of which we do not understand, big through bolts were used again. Extra strength was needed, and we must try to understand why.

A model (scale 1:10) was made, sufficiently complete to give us its undisputed shape. We then measured the model itself, and "took off" its lines, using the conventional shipbuilder's methods.

As far as we know, no one has yet applied the conventions of paper naval architecture to an ancient wreck. Neither is there much help from graphic or philological sources of this period, as the seventh century A.D., give or take a little, was not a time when enough people had enough money for enough city and house decorations, including ship representations on walls, vases, floors, or whatever, for any to survive through the accidents of history to instruct us about what to see in the Pantano wreck.

Lacking any such basis and taking lines directly from the model, we tried to draw as much of the ship as seemed correct.

Briefly, the point of the conventional drawing of ships' lines, whether to build a ship or to record the shape of an existing hull, is that a ship must be constructed with a system of fair curves, curves that can be drawn by the builder or reconstructor by a batten, stiff or flexible, in a mold loft or on the drawing board, through a series of points.

The points are derived—that is, noted, ticked off—in three principal sets of lines which inform us of the shape of a ship. If in the drawing of any of these lines there is a hitch, a nick, a crookedness, that means a crookedness or gouge occurs in the side of the ship; our lines are wrong; we must find the error.

One set of lines is the waterlines, which appear on the drawing as if one took each layer of a ship-shaped sandwich, horizontal from midships to the outer hull, and traced it on paper.

The second is the diagonals, lines drawn at useful intervals from the midships line at a downward angle to the outer hull, more or less at a forty-five-degree angle to the hull planking. This shows the angle at which water flows past the hull. We have found the diagonals the most useful for determining the relationship of the ship's section drawing to the shape of the hull as a whole. If the diagonals, drawn on plan, are not fair, the ship has a gouge in it somewhere, and it won't sail. The diagonals are particularly useful in dealing with the hull of a wreck.

The third group of lines is the buttock lines. If a knife is sliced through the ship from top to bottom, fore to aft, first near the midships line and then at intervals proceeding outward to the sides of the hull, and this slice of ship is then traced onto paper, that will be the buttock lines.

We worked from the model with a series of sections, taken at points indicated on the drawings, which were, as far as we could tell, the relevant ones, where the shape of the ship changed and where construction was singular and indisputable.

Working from the sections, we then drew the profile with bulwarks, waterlines, the reported length of ship and height of stempost, and the known position of cuts in frames and floors for the keel. At the same time, checking back and forth between the three drawings (section, profile, and plan), we drew the deck plan, with bulwarks and waterlines drawn out as if seen from above. (Waterlines are in this case a draftsman's convention of convenience, arbitrary reference lines drawn horizontally across the profile, transferred as curves to the plan.)

Here discrepancies occurred. There were indeed gouges and zigzags in our ship. Going back to the original data—that is to the excavation book with its plan of planking with all the nail holes after the frames were removed, and to the drawings of the many individual frames and other timbers—we checked out the sections to find possibilities of error. As we altered the sections slightly, one here, another there, the diagonals eventually came fair—that is to say, the ship became possible. She could float.

As we checked her out with fair curves, tightening her nail holes, she began to look somewhat less like a

saucer and more like a teacup. We tried hard to stand up the sides so that she looked like our idea of a ship.

Having returned to the excavation book, we then checked the new sections with the model, which indeed had been done with great care as to connecting nail hole to nail hole. Everything seemed all right, so far.

Then, out of curiosity, we discarded all the original data and drew sections from the plan, diagonals, and profile. This was a lengthy adventure, and the last. Sections drawn, we checked for a last time back to the model and the excavation log and found nothing wrong—that is, nothing contradicting the set of lines.

About a third of the ship exists. We know, from Salvatore Garifalo and other workers who saw much of the remainder of the ship before it was burned, the approximate length of the ship. Because a ship is necessarily built with fair curves, we think our reconstruction must be safe through, and a bit past, the midships section.

A large Byzantine cargo ship went ashore at Pantano Longarini in south Sicily fifteen hundred years ago. The area gradually silted up, and the original beach line is now five hundred yards from the sea. Workers digging an irrigation ditch in 1964 found and destroyed half the ship, after trying to sell the well-preserved timber to a local shipyard. In 1965, Gerhard Kapitän and the author excavated what was left. From top to bottom: Parts of the ship are covered with wet canvas to prevent them from drying out. The huge timbers—remains of the stern and starboard side of the ship—once supported a high stern structure. Joe Reinhardt photographs a detail of the construction.

The reconstruction was more difficult than we had expected. Working out the drawing was complicated but possible. What the drawing of the wreck told us, however, was exactly that—what the *wreck* looked like. What we wanted to know was what the *ship* had been like, and the 1:10 model was constructed.

We knew where frames and floors had been fastened. We had sections of the four which remained intact and many of the shorter ones higher in the ship, and could of course assume that the missing port side had been, for practical purposes, identical with the starboard. The keel was missing, but cuts in both frames and floors showed where it had been. Fastenings of the long interior stringers gave us an additional check on the shape of the hull below the waterline. Each time we made an error of arithmetic or carpentry, the nail holes were able to set us right again.

We soon found that honesty was not only the best but the only practical policy. Whenever we stretched points in order to make likely-looking pieces fit, we found that our mistake compounded itself. The first model had to be discarded completely, and we managed a satisfactory reconstruction with the second only after taking it apart and reassembling it several times.

Our policy during the excavation had been to record and measure everything, and special care had been taken to locate with all accuracy such things as nail and bolt holes. All the wood was soft on the surface, and much of it was in extremely delicate condition; we intended to move it, as we did, to a storage tank where fresh water would prevent its further disintegration, but we knew that the best and, always assuming the possibility of accident in transport, perhaps only opportunity of accurate recording lay in measurements taken while the wreck was intact as a whole.

The account of Salvatore Garifalo of Pachino, who was the mechanic in charge of the pump which kept the ditch dry for the bulldozer when the wreck was found, should be considered. Garifalo describes how the bulldozer struck wood, and he has a clear memory of what must have been the stem post being ripped clear by the bulldozer. Garifalo's recollections, the pieces left scattered afterward, and the excavation itself illustrate that what was originally *in situ* was the stem and stern of the ship, and the starboard side down to the waterline wale.

The width of the ditch, and Garifalo's clear recollection of the location of the stempost in relation to it, indicate that the over-all length of the ship on deck without projections was about thirty meters. This estimate fits the projection from the model very nicely. We have therefore made our tentative reconstruction of the ship as follows:

LOA 30·30 meters
LOD 29·45 meters
Length of keel 23·20 meters

Minimum possible draft light 1·50 meters; maximum draft loaded, 3·50 meters; gross tonnage, between 400 and 500; seagoing cargo capacity, over 300. We would not wish to claim that our conclusions about the size and shape of the Pantano wreck are other than well-worked-out assumptions.

Garifalo's most startling discovery was a plaque with Greek letters and a horse's head above the letters, about 1·20 meters long, attached to what must, from his description, have been a wale. I asked him if he knew Greek. He replied that he knew nothing about Greek, but that he remembered some of the letters. He described the plaque as being "metallic and banana colored." Could this have been gilt? He said it burned when it was put in the fire.

He tried, without me, to draw the letters he remembered.

I then made some experimental combinations of Greek letters in the notebook, attempting to work in

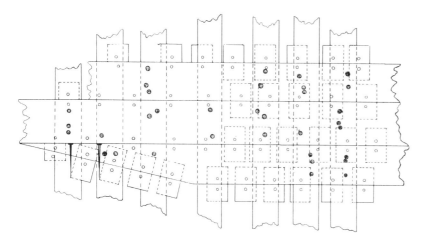

Drawing of the Torre Sgarratta ship. Copper fastenings were driven in without treenails—apparently as a late repair.

Hull of the Kyrenia ship reassembled in Crusader Castle at Kyrenia.

such a way that he would not be influenced. It was obvious that at some point in the conversation I began influencing him, though I tried hard not to do so.

As my knowledge of Greek leaves much to be desired, I propose no opinion, except that I am truly convinced that the mysterious piece of banana-colored wood was the ship's gilt nameplate, that it indeed had a small horse's head above the letters, that there were about six Greek letters. One fact will affect eventual interpretation of Garifalo's information: inscriptions on Roman lead anchor stocks seem to be the names of ships of gods. They are often misspelled.

The best possible evidence for dating is the construction, which seems to be in the same tradition as the early-seventh-century Yassi Ada ship. Although later evidence might well prove me wrong, I would date the loss of the ship to sometime after 500 A.D., with the remote possibility that the ship could have been lost just before the Arab invasion of Sicily. The best guess is, I think, perhaps 600 to 650 A.D., which fits the shards, the construction, the radio carbon date, and the historical data.

Conclusions

Most Roman and late Roman ships appear to have been double ended, and the Pantano wreck is the first ship excavated which has a transom stern. It seems likely that the heavy beams which sat on the waterline wale and extended aft from it were designed to support a large after cabin.

The Pantano ship probably came from the east, as cypress and pistachio wood are more typical of Aegean construction than of Italian. For instance,

Archangel, the sailing type of Greek schooner that we used at Torre Sgarrata, was built of cypress on mulberry wood frames. It seems likely that she was manned by Greeks, as she certainly had a Greek name. She was a large ship, with shallow draft for her size. She was undoubtedly seaworthy, but not so efficient to windward as other types of late Roman ships, like the Yassi Ada ship or the Mahdia ship, which had steeper floors.

Carpentry work is definitely transitional, a step between the beautifully built, copper-fastened full-tenon ships of the empire, and the "frame first" carvel-built caulked ships of medieval and modern times. The pistachio wood tenons are vestigial. Like those in the Yassi Ada wreck, they are set in large mortices quite far apart (in the Pantano wreck at intervals of about one meter), and they are not held in by treenails. This must be because they functioned only as a convenience to the carpenter in setting up the immersed part of the hull by the "shell first" method.

The men who originally found the wreck say that they saw the whole starboard side, including the stempost, but are certain that nothing existed below the waterline wale.

This means that the ship, probably heavily laden, might have struck a bar off the beach, trying to make the existing harbor, and broken in two. The bottom, cargo, and port side probably stayed on the bar. The starboard side broke off in one piece and washed ashore, to be covered up by sand and lie intact for us to study, 1300 or so years later.

Problems

This excavation, in a remote part of Sicily, poses several very serious problems.

The wood, after having been removed from the site, was put into Francesco Spatola's irrigation tank, where it could soak in fresh water until we could remove it for preservation.

Optimistically, we imagined that we would find funds for removal of the wood to permanent storage tanks where it would be intensively studied. The excavation had, in any case, to be made, or the ship would have been altogether lost during the construction of the drainage ditch. (There was a possible third alternative—that of the site having been marked by the Italian Archaeological Service as an archaeological site, stopping the reclamation project by Mr. Spatola, and doing nothing to increase the already minimal goodwill between the country people who find achaeologically important objects and the Archaeological Service which must deal with recovery, rewards, and restoration).

At this writing, eleven years have gone by since we excavated the Pantano and optimistically stored the pieces in Mr. Spatola's tank. We have never been able to raise the money to save the remnants of the ship.

It remains, in my mind, a moot question as to whether we should have excavated the Pantano or not. If we had not excavated her, she would have most probably been destroyed anyway. At the very least, we produced a reasonably good record of a ship of a forgotten type from a little-known period of seafaring. The beautiful timber of the Pantano ship has turned to dust, bulldozed, perhaps, or stacked and dried out. This record, laboriously made, will live on, so long as libraries last.

Treasure Diving and Politics

Various legal controls over undersea antiquities have been attempted, though few with successful results. In the Mediterranean, where I have worked for eighteen years, I have seen the development of several systems meant to preserve archaeological shipwrecks. Certainly there are many more wrecks in that area of the world than in the United States, and the dateline dividing salvage from archaeology, though often put somewhere in the nineteenth century, extends much further into the past.

Nearly all the Mediterranean countries have serious antiquity problems, on land as well as in the sea. Illegal exploitation is rampant. In districts where local authority does show concern, there is a good deal of hope, but in areas where archaeological appointments are governed by pork-barrel politics, the situation is desperate. Unlike the United States, most of these countries have an archaeological service, often on a ministerial level, staffed by trained archaeologists and financed by the government. Unfortunately, in the allocation of funds, archaeological services always seem to get the leanest portion. This situation should not exist in the United States, where antiquities are relatively rare and where much more money exists for this type of work.

The French have had among the worst of troubles with antiquities in the sea. Their southern coast was the first to be invaded by skin divers, beginning in 1947 when the aqualung caught on there. Literally hundreds of shipwrecks were found. The government, the navy, and a number of archaeologists and divers did all they could to control the large-scale looting, but by now nearly all the visible wrecks in depths more than one hundred and sixty-five feet have been completely destroyed. The same applies in Italy, where there are too many skin divers with little respect for archaeological services.

Greece and Turkey have laws regarding marine antiquities, but their problems are similar to those in

Italy and France. Enforcement is impossible. As tourism grows and more local people learn to dive, the portable remains of shipwrecks will fast disappear.

The problem is further acerbated by what might be called the culture gap between the local authorities and the skin divers. The European educational system is much more rigid than that of the United States. Archaeological service personnel tend to be library-oriented classicists. Divers are geared toward machinery, adventure, athletics, and romance. Several excavations of great promise failed because of the inability of one group to communicate with the other.

Professor Nino Lamboglia, one of the founders of marine archaeology, actually forbade his assistants to dive during an underwater excavation. He thought diving was a dangerous, undignified pursuit best left to the less gentle classes.

Yugoslavia is about the only country to have solved the problem. After a series of unfortunate experiences in the 1950s, the Yugoslavians have virtually forbidden skin diving of any kind. Yachts and diving equipment are sealed by Customs. This kind of control is possible in an authoritarian state but difficult in countries where freedom of the seas is a tradition.

Israel, too, is in reasonably good shape in regard to this problem, but Israel is a small country, its standards of education very high, its Mediterranean coastline only one hundred and seventeen miles long, and divers and archaeologists often know one another personally. Indeed they are, in some instances, the same people. There is a vigorous program to instruct divers and historians in the techniques of marine archaeology. Here too, surplus artifacts are drawn, photographed, numbered, and sold through the archaeological service to purchasers, either private individuals or museums. This is a good solution to an old problem: one good example of an amphora from the wreck of a wine-carrying ship, for instance, is enough for one museum. The biggest museum in the world has no use and probably no storage facilities for another thousand or so identical amphorae. The sale of objects, whose location is then known, in case they are needed for study, produces money which is then used for further museum or excavation studies.

Laws must be made that are strong enough to protect the sites, yet that are not so prohibitive as to be unenforceable and, therefore, virtually useless.

A state law regarding marine archaeology should probably accomplish several things: make it impossible for any group or person to rob any wreck and get away with it; reward anyone who helps the state preserve or excavate wrecks; and encourage supervised undersea research. Supervised undersea research can be accomplished only by creating a state or government department of marine archaeology (in the United States, Texas and Florida have done so with success). If such a department was established, perhaps a commission consisting of representative divers, historians, and educators could then be formed. The commission could decide which wrecks should be protected by the state and which could be awarded to commercial salvage companies. The commission budget should allow research into the problems of legislation, in order to recommend suitable legislation.

It should be brought to the attention of the legislators that wrecks given to commercial salvage companies, whether or not they are intended for "archaeological" salvage, will be destroyed. No commercial salvager has yet seen that material was properly studied or published, either in Europe or in America. There is a limit to the time available for lawmaking; too much delay will lose the state's heritage of marine objects.

If the wrong kind of legislation is made, and a situation arises in which skin divers and archaeologists are set against one another, then it is equally sure that the shipwrecks will be lost, just as they were in France. The wrecks must be saved now—or never. Their fate is partially in the hands of the lawmakers.

Afterword

At the edge of the Antarctic continent, overlooking the Great Ice Barrier, stands a large cross made of Australian jarrah wood. It is a memorial to Robert Falcon Scott and to the four men who died with him in 1912. On it is engraved a line from Tennyson's *Ulysses:* "To strive, to seek, to find, and not to yield."

Scott was seeking a treasure far grander than Spanish gold, a treasure that had value only in the imaginations of knowledgeable men. The first Arctic and Antarctic explorers dared these far regions for hope of commercial or political gain. Scott, and a dozen others of his heroic period, were heralds of a new age of discovery in the polar regions.

Marine Archaeology is a small enclave in the story of modern man's scientific exploration of the sea. There are treasures in the sea—unimaginable ones—from mineral nodules and galleons full of gold to sunken Russian submarines. Yet the true treasures of the sea are all noncommercial ones, in the narrow sense. Oceanography is not a commercial science, but the knowledge gained from oceanographic research can alter mankind's future. Knowledge of man's early sea explorations, of the ships and the men that sailed them, is an essential footnote to our understanding of ourselves. The remnants of John Paul Jones's *Bonhomme Richard* or those of a Cycladic ship of the early Bronze Age have no intrinsic value. Neither does the photograph of the doomed British polar explorers Scott, Oates, Wilson, Evans, and Bowers at the South Pole on January 18, 1912. After all, Roald Amundsen got there first.

Scott's motive was purely in the name of science. His Terra Nova Expedition was the first fully staffed scientific expedition to the Antarctic. But the South Pole visit was the "treasure," without whose allure the entire expedition could not have been financed.

In the twenty years since I became interested in ancient ships in the sea, I have experienced an interesting progression. When I first approached the editors of a national magazine with photographs of ancient ships on the sea floor, the first question put to me was, "Did you find gold?" In their minds, the only interesting aspect of a wreck was its treasure.

Eventually I traced the whereabouts of the Gelidonya wreck, which, up to that time, was the oldest shipwreck ever found. That discovery was spectacular enough to receive the support needed to excavate a Phoenician trading vessel of the thirteenth century B.C. Modern marine archaeology was, at last, launched. Unfortunately, we came full circle and ended again at the point where we had started when, in 1975, we found the Cycladic ship at Dhokos, Greece. Political pressure on the Greek Archaeological Service forced them to excavate the wreck with teams of untrained Greek Navy divers, who retrieved a heap of broken pottery and little else. Like Cinderella's jewels that turned to coal at the stroke of midnight, the oldest shipwreck in the world was reduced to junk by treasure hunters who were blind to the true treasure: a record of a seagoing vessel of four thousand years ago.

There are literally hundreds of underwater expeditions in progress throughout the world today. Most of them have been so distorted by the newspapers that it is very difficult to get an idea of what is really happening in the world of maritime archaeology. Those of us who are obsessed by what we think is the true treasure form a rather friendly group. Once a year or so we meet to exchange gossip about who is doing what. The last such meeting took place

A trade that has survived for at least three millennia, big clay storage jars are still transported for use in countries of the eastern Mediterranean. In ancient times the jars traveled by boat; this picture, taken in 1961, depicts one of the last cargoes to be carried in this manner. Today they travel by truck.

in Ottawa, Canada, in January 1977. Sponsored by the Indian and Northern Affairs and Parks Department of the Canadian government, it was an open meeting which any diver could attend for a small fee. I left the conference with an impression that what is going on in maritime archaeology today is both encouraging and daunting.

Amazingly, the countries furthest ahead in their work in maritime archaeology—that is, in underwater excavation—are Canada and Australia. The Western Australian Museum has a budget of perhaps three quarters of a million dollars per year for activities relating to maritime archaeology, a first-rate program in the field directed by Jeremy Green, and a modern conservation department. At present, they are working on five known East India ships that date from 1622 to 1727. In addition, Western Australia has instigated a Maritime Archaeology Act to protect its maritime archaeological heritage.

Canada's conservation lab in Ottawa is the most advanced in the Western Hemisphere. The 1967–1968 excavation of the *Machault,* a French frigate of the 1760s, brilliantly carried out by Walter Zacharchuk and Robert Grenier, prompted the Canadian government to support surveys throughout the country. Walter Zacharchuk and his team have seen some extraordinary wrecks in the Arctic, notably an almost intact schooner of the early 1700s. The icy waters of the far north and the far south seem to preserve ship timber, and modern diving suits, especially Swedish *unisuits,* allow diving in these frigid waters. Walter and I agreed to form a totally informal, unsponsored information exchange organization—POLARCH—for those enthusiasts interested in polar archaeology.

Dr. Daniel Nelson of the Royal Ontario Museum is developing a system whereby the intact American schooners *Hamilton* and *Scourge,* lost in Lake Ontario in 1812, will be rescued. He and his associates hope to raise each schooner in one piece and preserve them in refrigerated tanks of water, where they will be on public exhibition. The idea sounds incredible: after talking to Nelson I came away convinced that he and his group would be successful.

The freezing waters of Lake Ontario harbor hundreds of intact wrecks that date back as far as the 1600s. On the American side these wrecks are rapidly being destroyed by treasure-hunting skin divers. There is even a commercial company in Chicago that is searching for wrecks with side-scan sonar, and salvaging bits of them to be turned into coffee tables. No one in the states bordering the Great Lakes seems to care. In Canada they do: one of the most inspiring projects described at the meeting was the discovery of two nineteenth-century schooners near Prince Edward County in Lake Ontario by two dedicated women, Barbara M. Carson and Audrey E. Rushbrook of the Kingston (Ontario) Maritime Museum.

What is so wonderful about the two is that they are very feminine ladies of a certain age who completely destroy the macho image of the diver with knife strapped to his or her leg, swaggering around, daring the dangers of the deep. It is people like the Misses Carson and Rushbrook who are the hope of marine archaeology in the future.

Andre Lepin, of the Quebec Ministry of Culture, read a fine paper at the Ottawa conference, describing the recovery of objects from Admiral Walker's lost fleet of 1711. It seems that these wrecks are being saved from treasure hunters and carefully explored, and the finds are being preserved and placed in museums.

Compared to that in Canada, underwater archaeology in the United States is suffering. Although the National Trust for Historic Preservation started a maritime section in the fall of 1976, it seems that it will be some years before we have an operative national program whose aim it would be to preserve our historic shipwrecks. One problem in our country is that these matters are left largely to individual states. Some states, particularly Texas, have passed legislation that is sensible and constructive. The Texas Antiquities Committee has taken title to all historic wrecks in Texas waters, and has chosen a competent crew to work on them. The group is being led by Barto Arnold, who has successfully carried out a well-organized excavation of one of the wrecks of the Spanish treasure fleet that went ashore on Padre Island in 1554. The Texas State Laboratory for Archaeological Conservation is second to the Ottawa Lab in its careful and organized work on undersea archaeological finds on the continent. One day Texas will have a wonderful museum in which the finds from the 1554 fleet can be exhibited.

In contrast to the interest expressed in Texas, Florida has enacted a law that seems expressly designed to destroy ancient shipwrecks. The state contracts with private individuals to excavate historic shipwrecks within state-controlled waters. The finds are sent to the preservation lab in Tallahassee, where they are preserved and then divided between the state and the salvager. In short, the state has created a situation that practically guarantees the excavation of wrecks by commercial salvagers—not by archaeologists.

The most prominent of these companies, Treasure Salvors, Inc., of Satellite Beach, is currently salvaging the remains of the *Nuestra Señora de Atocha,* which sank near Marquesas Keys in 1622. The managing director of the company, Mr. Mel Fisher, began undersea salvage diving after opening a dive shop in California in 1954. Since then he has salvaged dozens of Spanish shipwrecks and has found and auctioned millions of dollars in gold doubloons and silver pieces of eight. Neither he nor anybody else in his organization has contributed very much to our knowledge of the Spanish in North America. As a profit-making venture, Treasure Salvors cannot avail itself of the funding and facilities available to legitimate archaeology. Shares in the company are owned by private individuals, who are in for a fling with tax-deductible money. Five people have been killed, including a close relative of Mr. Fisher. This is a large number of people, particularly when one recalls that the United States Navy's Man in Sea project was shelved because of the loss of one diver. But, because of the tragedies, Treasure Salvors is slowly coming around to accepting an archaeological, rather than a salvage, view of the Spanish treasure galleons: they have recently hired a staff archaeologist, Duncan Matthewson, who is struggling to turn their operation into something resembling an archaeological excavation.

What we are seeing in the United States in terms of marine archaeology is a historical progression, rather similar to the spread of museums throughout the country during the last hundred years. The great museums of New York and Boston were started in 1870. In 1900, there were about five hundred museums in the United States. Today there are about twenty-five hundred, with an aggregate operating income of some twenty million dollars—a far cry from the four-thousand-dollar-per-year operating income of the Smithsonian Institution before 1870. The National Trust for Historic Preservation was founded in 1949—only then did the government begin to deal with the accelerating destruction of our national architectural heritage.

The first real United States excavation of a ship, based on the standards of modern archaeology, began in Maine in the summer of 1976. A privateer brig of the American Revolution, the *Defense,* was burned in a sheltered inlet of the Penobscot in 1779 by her crew in order to escape capture by the British Navy. She was found in 1973 by a task force organized by the Maine State Museum, which included George Bass's American Institute of Nautical Archaeology and the Maine Maritime Academy. In June and July of 1976, the group, directed by Professors David Switzer of the University of New Hampshire and David Wyman of the Maine Maritime Academy, excavated the bow area of the ship. They found the bosuns' and carpenters' lockers, and began a site plan which will one day allow construction of a sailing replica. It is no coincidence that David Switzer learned to dive with George Bass at Yassi Ada, Turkey.

The techniques for work on very old ships that were developed by Americans in the Mediterranean have finally returned to their mother country. Historians of technology maintain that the technique of constructing, say, a complicated machine—the secret plans, so to speak—are not the key that would make it possible for scientists to construct hydrogen bombs, moon rockets, mini submarines, or, if one reaches further back into history, wheels, boats, or pyramids. What counts is the knowledge that such things are possible, that they have been built somewhere, and that they work. Man is an ingenious creature: once an idea is unleashed, it travels around the world. The *Defense* project has unleashed an idea in the United States: that the treasure of shipwrecks is their evocation of the memory of an important part of our past. The Air and Space Museum of the United States National Museum in Washington, D.C., exhibits the history of American aviation from the Wright brothers to the most detailed and the largest space rocket, by exhibiting the actual aircraft or replica. Someday we shall see ships exhibited in similar fashion.

The ships are there, waiting. Ericsson's *Monitor* (of *Monitor* and *Merrimac* fame) has been found by Harold Edgerton's side-scanning sonar off Cape Hatteras, where she has lain since 1863. So has a less renowned Civil War vessel, the gunboat *Hatteras*, which was sunk off Galveston the same year by the Confederate raider *Alabama*. She was discovered two years ago by a group of Houston divers. The *Hatteras*, all two hundred feet of her, lies under a protective shroud of mud in sixty feet of water. The Galveston Historical Foundation is now seriously considering salvaging, preserving, and exhibiting the *Hatteras*.

We still have a long way to go. My desk is full of rumors, sad stories of destruction and potential destruction. Captain James Cooke's ship, the *Endeavor*, may have been found during the winter of 1976 on a beach in Waverly, Rhode Island, where the winter gales have uncovered her. Despite the winter, souvenir hunters were already picking apart the wreck. A Revolutionary War frigate is suffering the same destruction by skin divers on Long Island. At the same time, a British sloop of war, also of the Revolution, is being eyed by a salvage contractor in Maine. The 1614 wreck of the Dutch *Tyger* seems to have been destroyed when the World Trade Center was built in New York City in 1967. The last intact American sailing cargo schooners of the end of the age of sail are rotting to pieces in Wiscasset, Maine. Yet, there is hope in the United States.

England is in better shape, in the sense that there is a growing national feeling of responsibility about historical shipwrecks. The British legal position is much better than that of the Americans, in that an act of Parliament has been passed allowing for "scheduling" of wrecks and their preservation from marauding divers. The British Sub Aqua Club has instituted a policy of training divers to respect the past. Alan Bax, a retired Royal Navy officer, has been running a training center for nautical archaeology for some years in Plymouth. Throughout England, dedicated little organizations, operating in the Robert Falcon Scott tradition, are doing serious scientific work with old ships. Among the protagonists are Colin Martin in Scotland, Alexander McKee in Portsmouth, and the indefatigable Sidney Wignall of Spanish Armada and *Bonhomme Richard* fame, who is setting out in the summer of 1977 to find the wreck of a mid-nineteenth-century 100-gun ship, the *Royal James*, sunk off Lowestoft.

England, in fact, has the first journal on the subject of nautical archaeology—*International Journal of Nautical Archaeology and Underwater Exploration*. Founded by Joan DuPlat Taylor, it is a treasure trove of reports on the field of ship archaeology. In its pages the total amateur diver, the little fellow with an aqualung, a wet suit, and dreams, will find a standard to which he can measure up. Here the professional will find a forum. The journal publishes reports on what is happening everywhere in the world in the field of marine archaeology.

The journal is also a continuity of dreams. In 1960, Joan DuPlat Taylor, George Bass, and I were together on a beach at Cape Gelidonya, dreaming of the day that such a publication would pull together the scattered skeins of communication in this very new field. George and I thought that there would never be enough material to fill a publication that would appear quarterly. Joan proved us wrong.

Sweden has produced the most spectacular treasure of all: the *Vasa*, a warship that sank as she was setting out on her maiden voyage from the Stockholm harbor. The *Vasa* project is largely the creation of the brilliant Swedish conservationist-engineer Lars Barkman, who has spent half a working lifetime preserving the ship. Besides his work on the *Vasa*, his lab has become a center for a new, advanced technology in the conservation of ancient wood, paper, metal, and cloth retrieved from the sea. Barkman's work on the *Vasa* has shown once and for all that a sunken ship can be saved and exhibited by a nation willing to do the job properly. His work has carved the path that will be followed in the future. The ships are there, and the determination to save them is growing in an ever-increasing number of countries.

The Danes have done marvelous things with their heritage of sunken treasures. Ole Crumlin Petersen's Roskilde Museum has become a center for the hundreds of people who are fascinated by the saga of man's conquest of the sea. Here, several groups have found the inspiration and technical data needed to construct excellent replicas of Viking ships, ships that have laid open to modern students the secrets of their voyages. The Roskilde Museum is also a center for divers, who are systematically exploring Danish waters for ancient shipwrecks. The three-mast schooner *Fulton*, salvaged by the museum association from a scrap heap, has been rebuilt and re-rigged, and now offers cruises to various Danish youth groups. The *Fulton* is doing her part to preserve the memory of a tradition that is almost gone, even in Denmark.

Finland and Norway have not succeeded as well as Sweden and Denmark, despite the efforts of a handful of dedicated individuals. The reason for this is probably that these countries have serious economic problems and a very recent sailing-ship tradition. It is difficult to convince an official whose father sailed in a ship of the last century that the ship is a historical object.

This "noninterest" appears to apply to Greece as well, a country where one of the oldest of the world's nautical traditions is quickly disappearing, without any record, and where folk memories of centuries of voyaging are being eradicated by the inevitable modernization of the country. Like the state of Florida, the Greek Government has settled on policies that one might imagine were designed purposely for the destruction of Greece's nautical heritage. No scholar has recorded the dialects of divers like the men of Symē who carried out the Antikýthēra excavation a long lifetime ago. The Antikýthēra wreck itself has been violated by a combination of politics and greed, most recently by Jacques-Yves Cousteau, who is working with the support of the Greek Government but without any competent archaeological staff. Newspaper articles of 1976 and early 1977 were full of Cousteau's treasure discoveries in Greece.

Regarding its marine antiquities, Turkey is in better shape than Greece, although the situation there is desperate. Legitimate diver-scholars are discouraged, while irresponsible wreck robbers are encouraged by default.

It seems clear that there will be few visible underwater antiquities left in either Greece or Turkey within a few years' time. Italy is stripped. An inadequately financed and hopelessly bureaucratic archaeological service in Italy cannot cope with finds on land, much less under water. France has gone through a very difficult period of outrageous destruction of its maritime antiquities, but there is a strong movement to reverse this.

The great hope of marine archaeology in the eastern Mediterranean was Michael Katsev's excavation and restoration of a merchant cargo ship of the fourth century B.C. at Kyrenia. This was a perfect example of a well excavated, perfectly preserved, and beautifully exhibited ship—and a true example of turning undersea trash into treasure. The Kyrenia shipwreck excavation was well on its way to becoming the spiritual and technical center of marine archaeology in the eastern Mediterranean when, in the summer of 1974, the Turks invaded Cyprus, effectively putting an end to the work. The ship was not damaged, and still survives in its air-conditioned hall in the Crusader Castle, but no tourists go to Kyrenia any more.

One tragedy of the political situation on Cyprus is that it has set both Greeks and Turks against the Americans, depriving both countries of American science and know-how, especially in marine archaeology.

In the thirty years since aqualung diving caught on in a big way, a great deal of treasure has been turned to trash. Very little real treasure has been found: the sea is a very large place. The Sunday newspaper supplements will always have a larger readership than the journals of underwater exploration, and the general public will always thrill to the wonderful idea of treasure in the sea. But in spite of all the scandals and stupidities, we are coming into a new period of underwater exploration, where even the most commercially minded of treasure hunters are beginning to realize that the value of shipwrecks goes far beyond the cash value of their sunken gold. Davy Jones's locker is wide open, full of magic things to those who are able "to strive, to seek, to find, and not to yield."

To those who merely wish to get rich, I can only recommend the roulette wheels of Monte Carlo. There, the odds are better.

Bibliographical Note

In devising a bibliography an author must choose between a technical, lengthy list of books that would probably not be very useful to the average reader, or only a few references. To me it seems impractical to reprint material that is easily available in any well-organized library. Assuming, then, that a reader of this book is sufficiently inspired to go to a library and dig a bit, I would advise him to proceed as follows:

Go right through the issues of the *International Journal of Nautical Archaeology and Underwater Exploration.* Published in England, this quarterly provides an excellent picture of what is going on in the field. It also includes authors' addresses, so you can choose the projects that interest you and write to the people involved.

Sea History, the journal of the National Maritime Historical Society (2 Fulton Street, Brooklyn, N.Y. 11231), also appears four times a year and contains news of the ship-preservation movement in the United States.

A History of Seafaring Based on Underwater Archaeology, edited by George Bass, includes articles written by thirteen specialists in the field, and an excellent bibliography. It was published in 1972 in London by Thames and Hudson and in New York by Walker & Company, and has been translated into French, German, and Italian.

William Bascom's *Deep Water, Ancient Ships* (Doubleday & Company, New York, 1976) provides an idea of what we could do if money were available and local politics allowed it.

My own *Shipwrecks and Archaeology* (Atlantic Little Brown, Boston, 1969, and Victor Gollancz, London, 1970) is a review of the whole problem, which is as valid today as when I wrote it in the mid-1960s.

Colin Martin's *Full Fathom Five* (The Viking Press, New York, 1975) includes a succinct Armada bibliography and provides a good description of what has happened to Armada wrecks in the United Kingdom.

Richard Gould-Adams' *The Return of the* Great Britain (Weidenfeld and Nicolson, London, 1976) deals with a totally different kind of problem, one that has nothing to do with diving, but the book offers a fascinating story of archaeological salvage.

Acknowledgments

Dozens of people have inspired me and helped me to understand undersea exploration. All of them have contributed greatly to this book. There are several names, however, that I would like to mention.

The late Julius Motal, photographer and expert photographic technician, developed what in some cases were very poor negatives so well that they came out as beautiful photographs in spite of my technical incompetence as a photographer. His son, Julio, carries on in his father's grand tradition.

If Kimo Courtenay had not taught me to dive with the aqualung twenty-five years ago, I would never have gotten involved in diving for underwater archaeological treasure.

Without the stimulation of Professor John Bullitt, we would not have done the work we did in Greece.

Much of the American work described in this book was done under the aegis of the University of Pennsylvania Museum because of the vision of Professor Freelich Rainey, who allowed George Bass to found the Museum's underwater archaeology section.

The late James Dugan and Professor Harold Edgerton helped raise the first ten thousand dollars that financed *Archangel* and *Stormie Seas*, and made many of our Mediterranean expeditions possible. Jimmy Dugan died the day before we sailed for Italy for the second season at Torre Sgaratta in 1967. If we ever have a research vessel dedicated to marine archaeology under the American flag, she should surely be named the *James Dugan*.

I have dedicated this book to Joan DuPlat Taylor, a lady whose difficult administrative work is turning marine archaeology from a treasure hunt into a disciplined *scientific* treasure hunt, and who has made honest men out of enthusiastic pirates.

Photo Credits

The author and the publishers wish to thank the following for their kind permission to reproduce the photographs and drawings that appear on the pages noted: **Norman Brouwer Collection:** pages 13 (top) and 14 (left); **Peter Clayton Collection:** page 80; **Harold E. Edgerton:** pages 57 (top left and right) and 59 (top); **Galveston Historical Society, Galveston, Texas:** page 15 (right); **Peter Goumain:** page 110 (top); **Kim Hart:** pages 35, 36, 40, 44, and 45; **Gerhard Kapitän:** pages 39 (top) and 99 (bottom); **Michael L. Katzev, Kyrenia Ship Project:** half title and title pages; **Susan Womer Katzev, Kyrenia Ship Project:** page 129 (bottom); **Klein Associates:** 57 (bottom left and right) and 59 (bottom); **Karl Kortum:** page 7; **Mariners Museum, Newport News, Virginia:** page 10; **National Geographic Society:** pages 78 and 85; **Peabody Museum, Salem, Massachusetts:** 9 (left); **John Stoddart:** page 33; **Teddy Tucker:** page 39 (bottom); **Diana Wood and Joan Throckmorton:** page 120 (top). All other photographs were provided by the author.

Index

A
Aeschylus, 68
Airlifting, 89, 91, 109–111
Aktarmades, 70, 73
American Institute of Nautical Archaeology, 41, 83, 114, 127
Amphorae, 30, 44, 45
Amundsen, Roald, 124
Andrea Doria, 25
Anoxia, 68
Antarctic, 26, 124
Antikythēra, 78–85, 87, 129
Aqualung, 14, 20, 30, 71, 73
Archaeology, underwater, 14, 16, 30–45, 54, 89, 105, 124–130
Archangel, 24, 26, 99, 121
Arnold, Barto, 127
Arras, Captain Kemal, 46, 75
Artemis, 52
Ashera, 89
Athénienne, 59

B
Barkman, Lars, 16, 129
Bascom, William, 131
Bass, George, 31, 42, 59, 78, 83, 87, 88, 101, 103, 104, 111, 114, 115, 127, 128, 129, 131
Bax, Alan, 128
Bends, 69, 71, 82
Benoit, Fernand, 30
Boats, diving, 24–25, 70, 79
Bodrum Marine Archaelogy project, 83
Bodrum Museum, 42
Bolsena, Lake, 108
Bonhomme Richard, 46, 56, 124, 128
Borjesson, Bengt, 112
Boutan, Louis, 22
Brea, Bernabò, 114
British Isles, 16
British Sub Aqua Club, 20, 128
Brunel, Isambard Kingdom, 18
Bullitt, John, 90, 105
Byrd, Richard E., 26

C
Caisson disease, 69
California gold rush, 13, 15, 16, 33
Calypso, 84
Cambrian, 62, 63, 65
Capa, Robert, 20
Cape Gelidonya expedition, 31–32, 37, 42, 87
Carson, Barbara M., 126
Champigny, 13
Charles Cooper, 15
Charles Morgan, 15
Cicero, 114
Clarke, Arthur, 50
Clipper ships, 13, 15
Coins, 48, 50, 62, 78, 88
Collingwood, Admiral, 65
Columbine, 87
Conrad, Joseph, 6, 15, 16
Cooke, James, 128
Cousteau, Jacques-Yves, 6, 20, 30, 31, 84, 129–130
Crawford, O. G. S., 30

D
Defense, 127–128
Demeter, statue of, 83
Determinée, 7
Dhokos, Greece, 56, 59, 61, 65
Diver, The (Kroton), 68
Divers, 68–77; skin, 16, 30, 122, 123
Diving, 20, 30; helmet, 68–70, 71, 75, 79; naked, 66, 68
Dumas, Frederic, 31, 54, 84, 103

E
Economou, A., 82
Edgerton, Harold, 55, 56, 57, 59, 128
Edwards, Henri Milne, 30
Egypt, 25
Elgin, Lord, 65, 79
Elissa, 15, 16
Endeavor, 128
Equipment, diving, 20, 23, 24, 68–70, 71, 75, 79
Evangelistria of Mykonos, 27

F
Falco, Albert, 50
Fennia, 13
Fisher, Mel, 127

Fjeld, 15
Flegel, Charles, 70
Florida, 47, 127
Flying Cloud, 15
Fulton, 129
Funding, 26

G

Gagnan, Emile, 20
Galveston Historical Society, 128
Garifalo, Salvatore, 118–120
Gear, diving, 20, 23, 68; basic, 24; helmet, 68–70, 71, 75, 79
Glafkos the Sailor (Aeschylus), 68
Glaucus, 66
Glory of the Seas, 13, 15
Gould-Adams, Richard, 131
Great Basses Reef, 22, 48, 50
Great Britain, 18, 131
Great Eastern, 18
Greek Archaeological Service, 44, 124
Green, Jeremy, 126
Grenier, Robert, 126

H

Hall, Alexander, 16
Hall, E. T., 55
Hamilton, 56, 57, 126
Hamilton, Gowan Edwin, 65
Hatteras, 128
Hayward, Jack, 18
Hellenic Institute of Marine Archaeology, 56
Helmet diving gear, 68–70, 71, 75, 79

I

Institute of Nautical Archaeology (England), 31
International Journal of Nautical Archaeology and Underwater Exploration, 129, 131
Irish, Clifford, 109
Italian Archaeological Service, 121

J

Jennsen, Victoria, 56
Jhelum, 15
Jones, John Paul, 124
Juvenal, 14

K

Kaiulani, 9, 11
Kalymnos, 66, 68–73
Kapitän, Gerhard, 99, 114, 116, 118
Karius, 111
Kartelias, Nikos, 23, 90
Katsev, Michael, 16, 130
Kingston (Ontario) Maritime Museum, 126
Kipling, Rudyard, 14
Klein, Martin, 56
Kointos of Smyrna, 68
Kondos, Dimitrios, 79, 81, 82, 83
Kortum, Karl, 9, 16, 18, 33
Kroton, 68
Kyrenia, 16, 120

L

Lamboglia, Nino, 30, 103, 111, 123
Larson, Karl Otto, 114
Lawhill, 16
Legal controls, 122–123
Lepanto, Gulf of, 55, 56, 57
Lepin, Andre, 126
Leveling, 104–105
Lightning, 15
Löfstrand, Jim, 56
Love, Robert E., 105
Lucian, 84

M

Machault, 126
Magnetometers, 55, 56, 59
Maine Maritime Academy, 128
Maine State Museum, 127
Mandalinci, 46, 75
Mangouros, Costas, 24
Martin, Colin, 128, 131
Mary Moore, 16
Mary Rose, 47
Matthewson, Duncan, 127
Mavrikos of Syros, 27
McKay, Donald, 13, 15
McKee, Alexander, 47, 128
Mead, Margaret, 46
Melville, Herman, 15
Menander, 68
Mentor, 65, 68, 78–79
Merrifield, 111
Methone, 66, 88–89, 100–105, 110
Michaelis, 82
Moby Dick (Melville), 15
Monitor, 55, 56, 128
Morison, Samuel Eliot, 15

N

Narcosis, 83
National Association of Underwater Instructors, 20
National Maritime Historical Society, 16, 131
National Museum of Athens, 41, 82, 83
National Trust for Historic Preservation, 126–127
Nautilus, 60, 62, 65, 78, 79
Nelson, Daniel, 56, 126
Nelson, Horatio, 31, 60
Niagara, 25
Niantic, 33
Nicholaides, Peter, 56
Nuestra Señora de Atocha, 127

O

Ocean Science Association, 26
Ontario, Lake, 56, 57, 126
"Operation Sail," 114
Otago, 15, 16
Owen, David, 84

P

Padre Island, 47, 127

135

Pantano Longarini, 114–121
Papadongonas, Alekos, 65
Parthenon, 65, 79
Pax, 16
Peterson, Ole Crumlin, 16, 114, 129
Petronius, 14
Photogrammetry, 108, 111
Photography, underwater, 20, 88, 111–113
Pinkham, Lydia, 26
Piraeus, 66
POLARCH, 126
Politics, treasure diving and, 122–123
Polly Woodside, 16
Porto Longo, 55, 87, 90, 91, 106
Poseidon, 41
Praxiteles, 84
Pressure, 20, 22

Q
Quaglia, Mr., 25

R
Reinhardt, Joe, 118
Research, 25
Riesenberg, Felix, 6
Rosencrantz, Don, 104, 111
Roskilde Museum, 129
Royal James, 129
Royal Ontario Musum, 56, 126
Rushbrook, Audrey E., 126

S
St. George, 87
San Francisco Maritime Museum, 9, 33
Sapienza Island, 100, 110
Schliemann, Heinrich, 16
Scott, Robert Falcon, 124
Scourge, 56, 57, 126
Sea Probe, 89
Seamanship, 6
Sebbe Als, 114
Shaw, Joseph, 109
Ship-preservation movement, 11
Ships, reconstruction of, 16, 30, 31, 32, 114–121
Skin divers, 16, 30, 122, 123
Snow Squall, 13, 16
Solla Price, Derek de, 84
Sonar, 55, 56, 57, 59
Souçoupe, 50
Sovereign of the Seas, 15
Spatola, Francesco, 114, 121
Sponges, diving for, 66, 68–75
Stadiatis, Elias, 79, 82
Stais, Spiridon, 82
Steffey, Richard, 114
Stenuit, Robert, 59
Stobart, John, 33
Stormie Seas, 24, 26, 27, 41, 47, 57, 81
Submersibles, 54
Sulla, 84
Surveying, underwater, 100
Switzer, David, 128
Symē, 66, 68, 69, 75, 79, 82, 129

T
Taillez, Philippe, 30
Taylor, Joan DuPlat, 31, 129
Teredos, 47, 50
Texas, 47, 127
Throckmorton, Joan, 45, 63, 106, 114
Torre Sgaratta, 26, 37, 91, 110, 114, 121
Treasure, 78–99
Treasure Salvors, Inc., 127
Tucker, Teddy, 41
Tyger, 128

U
University of Pennsylvania Museum, 31, 42, 46, 84, 88, 89, 114, 115
U. S. Navy Diving Manual, 20

V
Vailati, Bruno, 25
Van Doornink, Frederick, 78, 114
Vasa, 47, 112, 129
Vicar of Bray, 15, 16, 33
Villiers, Alan, 6
Vitruvius, 14
Vose, Terry, 54–55, 91

W
Wagner, Kip, 47, 84
Walker, Admiral, 126
Wallihan, Roger, 100, 105, 109, 110
Watt, Henry Fowler, 16
Western Australian Museum, 126
Whale, Lesley, 56
Wignall, Sidney, 55, 56, 128
Wilson, Mike, 48
Wrecks, 6, 7, 14, 16, 25, 30, 31–32, 41, 46–65, 78–99, 114
Wyman, David, 128

Y
Yalouris, Fred, 56
Yassi Ada, 46, 47, 78, 87–88, 101, 104, 114, 115
Youngman, John, 109

Z
Zacharchuk, Walter, 126
Zeus of Artemisium, 41